HONG KONG MANAGEMENT CASES IN HOTEL MANAGEMENT

HONG KONG MANAGEMENT
— CASES IN —
HOTEL MANAGEMENT

Compiled and edited by

The Management Development Centre of Hong Kong

The Chinese University Press

The Management Development Centre of Hong Kong

ISBN 962–201–734–7

The Chinese University Press
The Chinese University of Hong Kong
Sha Tin, New Territories
Hong Kong
Fax: +852 2603 6692
E-mail: cup@cuhk.edu.hk
Web-site: http://www.cuhk.edu.hk/cupress/w1.htm

The opinions expressed in the cases of this book
are those of the authors, not of the MDC or
The Chinese University Press.

Printed in Hong Kong.

Contents

Preface

Realizing that there is a shortage of locally relevant management cases which could be used by trainers and teachers in Hong Kong, the Management Development Centre started to change this situation in 1987 by publishing the first English language edition of the case compendium in early 1989. Since then, three other case compendia have been published. The compendia have been widely used by various educational institutions which teach management in the territory. They are also proving useful to many of the training providers in Hong Kong, and to many companies using cases for in-company management training.

In order that management trainers can use the cases more effectively, in collaboration with The Chinese University Press, a series of Hong Kong case books which trainers can use in a classroom environment, will be published starting from 1996. Again, all the cases included in the series are local ones. They can form the core of a teaching or training session for a group and, of course, as projects or exercises to identify development needs.

We acknowledge the commitment and hard work of the many authors of these cases and those who carried out the technical review and editing of this case book.

The Management Development Centre
of Hong Kong
September 1996

Acknowledgements

We would like to acknowledge the contributions made by the teaching staff of the Department of Hotel and Tourism Management, Hong Kong Polytechnic University. We are grateful for the help of Mr. William Hsu in coordinating the writing of the cases. His case, "An Anatomy of a Hotel Closing — The Case of Hong Kong Hilton," is also the winning case of the 1995 Case Writing Competition.

The cases in this book are drawn from a number of sources and any resemblance to existing companies is coincidental.

Introduction

What is a "case study"? It is a representation of reality. Usually, it is a problem taken from real life. Indeed, all of the cases in this book are based upon events that actually happened in Hong Kong.

Each case should contain sufficient background data for students to identify the issues and put forward proposed solutions. No case can, by its very nature, contain all the information needed for a perfect decision. However, that is itself like the world in which the practising manager has to live. Most managers operate in conditions of incomplete knowledge and can never be sure about the impact of their decisions. Moreover, decisions seldom prove to be "right" or "wrong." The situation that a manager faces is seldom that clear-cut.

Tackling a Case

If you are a student faced with a case study for the first time, this may look a pretty daunting task. You may be at a loss to know where to start. The guidelines below are by no means comprehensive but you should find them useful.

Step 1: Groundwork

Read the case through quickly to give yourself an idea of the "big picture." Re-read the case, marking what you consider to be the key areas or the areas about which you are uncertain.

Step 2: Problems

After a third reading, list down what you see as the main problem areas. Prioritize these problems:

1. Which are the most important?
2. Which are having the biggest impact and why?
3. Which demand the most immediate attention and why?

Step 3: Analysis

1. How did the problems occur? What are the causes?
2. Do not fall into the trap of confusing symptoms with core problems.
3. Where you do not have sufficient information, make assumptions that you can rationally defend.
4. Most fundamentally, are all these problems actually capable of solution?

Step 4: Alternatives

Most problems can be tackled and "solved" in a number of different ways. Generate possible courses of action and test them by asking yourself:

1. How many of the problems will this solve?
2. To what extent will they be solved?
3. Will this solve the most important, most basic problem(s)?
4. What resources will this course of action require? Are they available?
5. Are there any disadvantages to this solution? What are the risks?

Step 5: Action

Which course of action is the "best"? Be sure that you are explicit about what makes it "best." Is it speed, economy, acceptability?

Draw up your plan answering these questions:

1. *What* is going to be done?
2. *Who* is going to do it?
3. *When* is it going to be done and what are the stages along the way?
4. *How* is it going to be done? Set down the detail of your approach.
5. *Why* is it going to be done that way?

If you follow these steps and can answer these questions, you are probably well on the way to an effective case solution.

Step 6: Confirmation

A useful check, when you have completed your work on the case, is to go through the following process.

Findings	Conclusions	Recommendations
1.	1.	1.
2.	2.	2.
3.	3.	3.
4.	4.	
5.	5.	
6.		
7.		
8.		

1. List your findings, the information that you have gathered about the situation described in the case.
2. Write down your conclusions based on your findings. Each conclusion *must* be based on your findings. You cannot make conclusions that are not backed up by *facts*.
3. Draft your recommendations for action. Every one of your recommendations *has to be* supported by at least one of your conclusions.

In the diagram, Recommendation 1 is backed by Conclusion 1. However, Conclusion 1 is not based on findings. Hence, it is not being supported.

Part I

General Management

1

An Anatomy of a Hotel Closing — The Case of Hong Kong Hilton

William S. F. Hsu

Introduction

On 22 January 1994, the owning company of the Hong Kong Hilton Hotel, property tycoon Mr. Li Ka-shing's Hutchison Whampoa, publicly announced that they had bought out the remaining twenty years of management contract with the Hilton Group for US$125 million (about HK$965 million). The 26-storey, 750-room Hilton Hotel was the oldest "grand dame" hotel on the Hong Kong Island. It opened its doors in 1961 and has since been the favourite hotel for tourists and dignitaries alike. This landmark closed its doors on 1 May 1995 to be rebuilt as a multi-storey commercial office complex.

The announcement also included plans of Cheung Kong Holdings, Mr. Li Ka-shing's flagship company, to jointly develop Hilton's neighbouring sites — a private car park and Beaconsfield House, a property belonging to the Hong Kong government.

Like most employees who started their career when the hotel first opened, Mr. Wong, 35, a housekeeping department employee, did his last "turn down" service on the evening on 30 April. He, along with some of his fellow workers, was "officially retired" after that day. The hotel carried a total of 850 employees and many, like Mr. Wong, had been with the hotel for over fifteen years.

Mr. James Smith, the hotel's General Manager, said the buy-out was an unfortunate, but a logical, business decision: "As a hotel, it's worth $500 million; as an office block, it's [worth] $1 billion."

Most hoteliers have different opinions on the buy-out, but all agree that it is highly unlikely that another top hotel such as the Hilton, the Mandarin Oriental, the Furama or the Ritz-Carlton will be built in Central, Hong Kong.

Sadly enough, the Hilton Hotel was not the first hotel to be bulldozed. In October 1991, the 194-room Grand Hotel closed its doors in Tsim Sha Tsui, Kowloon to be demolished and rebuilt into a multi-story office tower. In 1993, the 20-year old Lee Gardens Hotel in Causeway Bay was knocked down to make way for a commercial office project. Similarly, the Ambassador Hotel, the China Harbour View Hotel and a host of others followed suit. It appears that a trend of epidemic proportion has been established for owners, developers, and investors who see that office accommodation is in greater demand, and who are pulling down hotels and redeveloping the sites into office buildings.

Table 1 presents a historical "checked in and checked out" of hotel supply from 1993 onwards.

Meanwhile, tourist arrivals in Hong Kong continue to increase. In 1994, it grew by 11.6% to 8.9 million visitors. Within the next ten years, the number is estimated to double. With the new Chek Lap Kok Airport underway and the Hong Kong Convention Centre under expansion, tourism and convention activities is going for a record level, generating $64.3 billion in 1994, the second largest foreign currency revenue earner for Hong Kong.

Hotels, traditionally, among all the real estate income-producing properties, are considered to be the most complicated, yet most glamorous and lucrative. The term "perpetuity" signifies that the going concern of that business is expected to last for ever. This is especially so in the hotel business.

In the world of hospitality, an annual city-wide hotel performance with occupancy percentage in the mid-1980s (like Hong Kong's) are rare and usually becomes the most envied city of all. Yet, a lot of hotels are approaching their final destiny.

What Gives Here?

In the closing of a hotel, there are numerous issues and rationale to

Table 1: Newly Built and Demolished Hotels since 1993

Period	Hotel	Rooms added	Rooms deleted	Balance
1993				
Jan.–March	Newton Hotel Hong Kong	362		
	Silvermine Beach Hotel	135		
June	Regal Hongkong Hotel	423		
	Lee Gardens Hotel		660	
	Fortuna Hotel		187	
	Eastern Valley		111	
	Po Hang		70	
Oct.	Ritz-Carlton Hotel	216		
Dec.	China Harbour View Hotel		310	
	Gold Coast Hotel	443		
	BP International House	536		
1994				
Jan.–March	China Merchant Hotel		285	
	The South China Hotel	204		
	Ambassador Hotel		313	
	Harbour Hotel		156	
June	Pearl Seaview Hotel	263		
July	Emerald Hotel		316	
Dec.	Peninsula Hotel Extension	150		
1995				
Apr.–June	San Diego Hotel	99		
	Victoria Hotel		536	
	Hong Kong Hilton Hotel		750	
	Total	2,831	3,694	−863

Source: Hong Kong Hotel Association.

be considered. In all, every aspect of management decisions, be it marketing, finance, human resources, investment, or government politics etc., will offer their fair share of consideration in such a drastic and complicated business decision.

This case should not be viewed as a hotel-related case only, but rather an expose of the rationale, external and internal factors that contributed to the ultimate decision: one of an executive management decision in a highly sophisticated world of business; one that ultimately not only affects the whole business or the entire hotel itself, but also confronts the entire Hong Kong hotel industry and perhaps the overall confidence and prosperity of a colony in transition.

The following paragraphs led some of the rationale of the closing. They are not Hilton-specific; any hotel owner, developer and investor will undoubtedly have contemplated these issues before arriving at the final conclusion.

Readers would formulate and build up their own sense of urgency as they consider both from a micro and macro point of view how the issues all come in to play and thus lead to the ultimate decision of tearing down a hotel and rebuilding it as a commercial office building.

Hotel and Guest-house Accommodation Ordinance

On 8 August 1988, an electrical fault sparked a blaze in the lower floors of the 16-story Mirador Mansion in Tsim Sha Tsui. A total of 327 residents and hostel guests were evacuated as dense smoke enveloped the building. A total of 320 firemen and 27 fire engines were deployed. Twenty-three people, including a baby girl, four elderly men, two elderly women and two firemen, were treated for smoke inhalation at the Queen Elizabeth Hospital.

Ironically, the Mirador is just two blocks away from Chungking Mansion, a block of some 170 guest-houses and businesses where a Danish tourist, Mogens Kijeldgaard Jensen, fell to his death trying to escape a fire. In this mansion, there are about 1,500 hostels ranging from a single-room investment to multi-story business. These hostels provide cheap and affordable accommodation for hundreds and thousands of tourists each year.

Since tourists from China have been allowed to visit Hong Kong, thousands have come to the territory looking for cheap, short-term accommodation. This has led to rapid growth of hostels and guest-houses.

Much like the Mirador Mansion, Chungking Mansion was originally built as a residential property. Since then, entrepreneur owners have renovated their individual premises from that of a residential unit into multi-unit hostels and guest-houses. In so doing, in-room electrical appliances such as televisions, air-conditioners, and lighting fixtures have substantially increased the power demand.

Using unlicensed electricians, the owners have foregone the installation of an expensive new transformer which would offer proper electricity loading to the entire building. With shoddy and improper wiring, safety devices were deemed useless and often overload of electricity would occur. Fires would break out when overload cables exploded causing short circuits.

Between August 1988 and January 1995, there were a total of 28 fires within Chungking Mansion itself; most were due to electrical short circuits and malfunction of cookers.

In September 1988, the Hong Kong government introduced the Hotel and Guest-house Accommodation Ordinance which requires hotels and guest-houses alike to be licensed by the Licensing Authority of the City and New Territories Administration and each license to be renewed every year. In addition, the proposed licensing fees would be changed from a traditional flat rate to a scaled scheme. This means the more rooms a hotel has, the higher the licensing fees. In general, hotels face a fee rise of as much as 13 times from the present annual rate of $24,000.

Apart from those posing an immediate fire hazard like the hostels in Mirador Mansion and Chungking Mansion, the authorities required all hotel operators to carry out remedial work to meet the safety requirements before September 1993.

This Ordinance drew fierce criticism from the Federation of Hong Kong Hotel Owners. "Under the new Ordinance," a spokesman from the Federation claimed, "almost all the recognized hotels in Hong Kong would fail to meet the new tougher restrictions. And remedial work would costs millions." For example, a new three-star hotel had to spend almost HK$7 million replacing doors with the more fire-resistant models.

Mr. Michael Li, executive director of the Federation, claimed that the Licensing Authority's list included some guest-houses which the hotel industry did not consider qualified to claim the title of a hotel; and that the Ordinance should only focus on the guest-houses and the hostels which should never have been considered as part of the hotel industry due to their shoddy structure and facilities with zero services.

Furthermore, Mr. Li said that the tourism industry of Hong Kong, which earns $63.4 billion a year, would be endangered by the licensing conditions because they are inflexible and ignorant of the hotel industry.

The Licensing Authority refused to offer such a "grandfather clause," i.e. to exempt those hotels that were already built and complied with building and fire regulations and codes when they were first constructed. Moreover, it claimed that it was impossible to exclude existing hotels from the Ordinance because it was exactly the purpose of the Ordinance to "license" all hotels to bring them in line.

Faced with the stringent conditions laid down in the new legislation, older hotels are likely to suffer most severely as they were not required to have a build-in sprinkler system when they were first built many years ago. To install such a sprinkler system, these hotels will have to demolish several upper floors to erect a water tank which would not only disrupt operations but would cost millions.

Thus we see from as early as 1988 the seeds of dissatisfaction and potential defection have been sown as a result of this continuing battle of Fire Ordinance between the Hong Kong government and the hotel owners.

This is just the beginning.

Labour Importation Scheme

One of the competitive advantages Hong Kong has enjoyed in the past has always been its abundance of labour and the low wages that resulted in cheaper goods, products and quality services. There were times when the ratio of employees to guest-room of a hotel was 2 to 1. Those were the times when labour costs were low and the cost of living was more affordable in Hong Kong.

Annual inflation has been around 9–10% for the last nine years. Compared with other developing countries such as China, Vietnam and

Cambodia, Hong Kong's labour wages are high and many industries (especially the manufacturing industry) have moved to China or elsewhere to capitalize a competitive lower wages.

Consequently, the economy of Hong Kong, compared with its heyday, has taken a downturn. Unemployment has become the highest in the last ten years and the cost of living is getting higher.

The government has introduced an Labour Importation Scheme that allows 25,000 "skilled" workers from foreign countries like Thailand and China to come to Hong Kong annually working in various industries, including the hotel sector.

This Scheme has been a hotly contested issue between employers and employees in every sector, especially in the hotel sector where the government has only allowed approximately 10% of its annual request.

From the hotel employers' point of view, it was felt that the quality and productivity of staff in Hong Kong, particularly in line positions, was low. The development of a qualified labour pool for the industry has not kept in pace with increases in demand. The overall consensus was that there was an urgent need for the government to increase the labour importation quota in the hotel sector.

Additionally, recent surveys done by employers of the sector indicated the exhaustive efforts that have been made to attract qualified local workers, but still in vain. Although many employees from other industries have switched to the hotel sector, unfortunately after some on-the-job training, they still do not measure up.

On the other hand, the Labour Importation Scheme was vehemently opposed by the Association of Hotel and Restaurant Employees. They claimed that as some of the hotels closed one by one, employees having been laid off would have difficulty in finding jobs in the same industry. The request of employers for more imported labour is only a move to hire cheaper labour under the name of quality upgrading in order to reduce their payroll and benefit expenses.

The employees claimed that through this Scheme the employers can save pension expenditure and other miscellaneous benefits to employees such as education and housing allowances. Employers can also save a sizeable amount of money after deducing the expenses for their accommodation.

Both sides sought help and political influence from the Legislative Council. In a re-election of political candidates for a seat in Hotel and Restaurant service sector within the Legislative Council in September 1995, it pitted the two most prominent persons within this sector campaigning fiercely for the only seat.

Mr. Chan Wing-chan, nominated by the Association of Hotel and Restaurant Employees with heavy union support, was leaning heavily towards the employees. The other candidate, Mr. Michael Li, the executive director of the Federation of Hong Kong Hotel Owners, was favoured by the employers.

Mr. Li is a graduate of a leading hotel school in North America, speaks fluent English and is conversant with the hotel business issues. Mr. Chan, on the other hand, does not speak English and has risen to his rank largely through union support.

By a relatively small margin, Mr. Chan won the seat in the Legislative Council. Shortly after, on 12 October, Governor Chris Patten announced that he would amend the Labour Importation Scheme in a supplementary quota and reduce the allocation from 25,000 to 5,000.

Hotel Operating Costs

Among all the real estate income-producing properties such as apartment, commercial offices and hotels, hotels have always been the most complicated. It is highly labour-intensive, highly competitive, service-oriented, and has a very cyclical nature with peak and valley seasons (a hotel room not sold for the night is an income cost).

Horwath Asia Pacific, a certified public accounting (CPA) and hotel industry consulting firm, has conducted a research on the trends of the hotel industry. It had surveyed various types of hotels: High Tariff A, High Tariff B, Medium Tariff, and hostels and guest-houses. The 1994 Hong Kong hotel industry percentage distribution of revenues and expenses are presented in Table 2.

As can be seen from Table 2, of all the operating costs of a prototypical hotel in Hong Kong, payroll (plus related expenses such as fringe benefits) and departmental expenses are usually the two highest category of expenses. These consume over 37% of the total

Table 2:　Hong Kong Hotel Industry Percentage Distribution of Revenues and Expenses, 1994[1]

	All hotels[2] (%)	High tariff A hotels (%)	High tariff B hotels (%)	Medium tariff hotels (%)	Hostels/ Guest-houses (%)
Department revenues					
Rooms	56.5	51.9	58.5	65.4	73.5
Food	25.6	29.3	23.5	19.1	18.5
Beverage	6.8	7.9	6.5	4.0	1.0
Other food and beverage	1.2	1.6	0.7	0.9	0.8
Telephone	3.8	3.2	4.4	4.3	2.1
Minor-operated	3.9	4.5	2.9	3.8	2.8
Rentals and other income	2.4	1.6	3.4	2.4	1.3
Total	100.0	100.0	100.0	100.0	100.0
Department expenses					
Rooms	11.7	10.2	11.9	15.4	20.5
Food and beverage	24.0	27.4	21.9	18.7	15.8
Telephone	2.1	1.8	2.4	2.5	1.5
Minor-operated	2.0	2.5	1.5	1.6	2.3
Total	39.9	41.9	37.7	38.2	40.0
Department profit					
Rooms	44.8	41.7	46.7	50.1	53.0
Food and beverage	9.4	11.4	8.7	5.3	4.5
Telephone	1.6	1.3	2.0	1.8	0.6
Minor-operated	1.9	2.0	1.4	2.3	0.5
Rentals and other income	2.4	1.6	3.4	2.4	1.3
Total	60.1	58.1	62.3	61.8	60.0
Undistributed operating expenses					
Administrative and general					
Payroll and related	3.8	3.0	4.4	5.0	4.8
Others	2.5	2.5	2.6	2.5	4.6
Total	6.4	5.5	7.1	7.5	9.4
Marketing					
Payroll and related	1.2	1.2	1.2	1.2	0.5
Others	2.5	3.1	2.2	1.4	0.4
Total	3.7	4.3	3.4	2.6	0.9
Energy costs	3.4	2.9	4.0	3.9	4.3
Property operation and maintenance	3.7	3.7	3.9	3.5	4.1
Total undistributed operating expenses	17.2	16.4	18.3	17.5	18.7
Income before management fees	42.9	41.7	44.0	44.3	41.3
Management fees [Base and incentive]	3.7	4.8	2.8	2.6	2.2
Income before fixed charges	39.2	36.9	41.2	41.7	39.1
Fixed charges	13.6	8.8	21.8	11.1	6.6
Income before taxes	25.6	28.1	19.4	30.6	32.5
Reserve for capital replacement	1.1	1.5	0.7	0.9	1.1

Notes:　1. All figures are means; 2. Does not include hostels and guest-houses.
Source:　Horwath Asia Pacific.

revenue while the income before taxes only amounts to approximately 26%.

Comparing these hotel expense percentages with the expenses of a commercial office complex, it can be seen that the management fees, the energy and utility bills, the security management charges, the heat, ventilation and air condition (HVAC) and other costs are generally being borne by the tenants. As a result, what the actual net rental income would most probably be the unencumbered profit to the owners.

Table 3, which is contributed by Pannell Kerr Forster, a hotel consulting company, denotes the comparison between operating a hotel and a commercial building development.

Table 3:   Development/Operating Comparison of Hotel and Commercial Building

Key variables	Hotel	Commercial building
Development costs	Luxury hotel, HK$1,195 per sq. ft.	Grade A (excluding land) per building, HK$990 per sq. ft.
Operating costs	Luxury hotel, 74%	Insurance, tax of gross revenue, maintenance expenses passed on to tenants
Years to reach	3 to 4 years	One year stabilized operation
Staff required for	1.6 person per room	Less than 40 operation persons for office of equivalent total floor area
Capital replacement	2–3% annually	2–3% every five years
Occupancy variance	Daily	2 to 3 years' lease terms
Payback period	8 to 12 years	2 to 5 years

Source: Pannell Kerr Forster Consulting Limited

These results may not totally convince any owners to make the drastic decision, but along with what have been presented so far, this would add on the sentiment leaning towards office in lieu of hotel.

Plot Ratio between Hotels and Commercial Office Buildings

Since the Summer of 1992, the office rental market in Hong Kong has been rapidly strengthening. From a low of HK$16 per square foot during 1991, rents in Exchange Square were $100 per square foot in 1995.

According to an office leasing expert, Jones Lang Wootton Limited, office rents increased 40% in 1993 alone and rose another 10% in the first two months of 1994. Given the demand, grade A office space is drastically in short supply, especially in Central where vacancy rate is around 2%. Average monthly rents in Central are now around $90 per square foot, one of the most expensive in the world.

Most real estate analysts see these commercial office rents will continue to rise and office space will be highly sought after, especially in prominent locations in Central.

The Hong Kong Hilton Hotel is located at 2 Queen's Road, the centre of Central District, and in a premier location with a relatively unobstructed harbour view.

Previously, under the Hong Kong Building and Planning Regulations, there was no land particularly zoned for hotel development and no special tax incentive for luring hotel developers.

Hotels are generally treated as domestic rather than non-domestic or commercial property. Domestic property has a plot ratio of 8 to 10 while non-domestic one has a plot ratio of 15. In the past, hotel developers were usually allowed to have a plot ratio of 10, which would include the basement and the engineering rooms, but they had to obtain the concessions from the government.

The granting of the plot ratio was actually calculated when the government decided to auction off the land. Systematically they looked into the density of population, sewage, and transportation in order to issue the plot ratio.

In terms of density, a residential unit usually has 2 to 3 people in a home dwelling while a hotel's room is a unique and separate quarter to house only the allotted guest(s) with the double occupancy rate usually between 1 to 2 persons.

The occupancy rate of a domestic household is full everyday of the year while the vacancy rate of a hotel is between 10% to 20% annually. In addition, many hostels and guest-houses are being used by those people who took them as apartment. When these people travel somewhere for business, the room(s) will remain empty. This is quite different from that of a standard domestic household. Judging from these types of discrepancies, it is actually more suitable the hotels to be redeveloped as commercial office buildings.

On a commercial site in Central, the market value of a grade A office is 3.5 times that of a high tariff A hotel such as Hilton, assuming $7,363 per square foot for the total office space. This is far different from the 9.25 capitalization rate for the income before taxes, debt and depreciation for a prototypical hotel on the same plot of land.

The expected higher return from commercial development places the hotels, including the Hong Kong Hilton Hotel, in a very disadvantageous position as there is no way that any hotel can compete with commercial office buildings.

No wonder hotel owners have been doing their sums. "You cannot blame the hotel investors," admits Manuel Woo, executive director of the Hong Kong Hotels Association, "but we are seeing an epidemic of hotels turning [into] commercial buildings and I am very concerned."

Seeing that there is no government help being rendered and with the existing economic situation favouring commercial office rental, logic dedicates that hotels are losing their appeal. It is definitely more advantageous to convert, tear down and rebuild hotel premises as commercial office buildings, until such time that a saturation or equilibrium of the supply and demand of the office rental is reached.

This is particularly so in Hong Kong where office space is among the most expensive in the world. It is unlikely that the office value will fall drastically or the hotel value will rise significantly in the same manner.

Knowing this, the Hong Kong government is slow to respond to take any action.

Question for Discussions

With an understanding of the background environment that lends itself to the trend of hotels being demolished in lieu of commercial office buildings, work out the cash flow situation of Cheung Kong Holdings in the rebuilding of Hilton Hotel. What is your own conclusion?

References

1. *Eastern Daily*, 19 May 1995, p. 17.
2. *Eastern Daily*, 12 October 1995, p. B1.
3. *Hongkong Standard*, 18 November 1991, p. 10.
4. *Hongkong Standard*, 22 April 1995, p. 9.
5. *Hongkong Standard*, 18 September 1995, p. H-3.
6. *Hongkong Standard*, 8 December 1995, Financial Review.
7. *Hong Kong Tourism Magazine*, Interview on Howard Yeung, April 1995.
8. Letter to Honourable Chris Patten, Governor of Hong Kong, Federation of Hong Kong Hotel Owners, 30 October 1993.
9. *Ming Pao*, 21 May 1995, p. D4.
10. *Ming Pao*, 8 October 1995, p. B3.
11. *Ming Pao*, 21 November 1995, p. 10.
12. *Ming Pao*, 30 November 1995, p. 11.
13. *Ming Pao*, 11 December 1995, p. B3.
14. Pannell Kerr Forster Consulting Limited, *Comparative Marketing Position*, pp. III–45.
15. *Sing Pao*, 20 September 1994, p. 12.
16. *Sing Pao*, 3 October 1994, p. 14.
17. *Sing Pao*, 7 October 1995, p. 10.
18. *South China Morning Post*, 8 August 1988, Fires.
19. *South China Morning Post*, 23 January 1994, p. 1 (Business)
20. *South China Morning Post*, 10 July 1994, p. 3 (Business).
21. *South China Morning Post*, 17 December 1994, p. 23.
22. *South China Morning Post*, 18 January 1995, p. 2 (Business).
23. *South China Morning Post*, 20 January 1995, p. 2 (Business).
24. *South China Morning Post*, 20 February 1995, p. 3 (Business).
25. *South China Morning Post*, 3 March 1995, pp. 1, 10 (Business).
26. *South China Morning Post*, 29 April 1995, p. 1 (The Review).
27. *South China Morning Post*, 9 September 1995, p. 9 (Business).
28. *South China Morning Post*, 15 September 1995, p. 1 (Business).
29. *South China Morning Post*, 26 September 1995, p. 8 (Business).
30. *South China Morning Post*, 3 October 1995, p. 2 (Business).
31. *South China Morning Post*, 13 October 1995, p. 4 (Business).

32. *South China Morning Post*, 12 December 1995, p. 8 (Business).
33. "Sic Transit the Glory That Was the Hilton," *Window*, 21 April 1995, pp. 14–15.

2

Full Metal Jacket

William S. F. Hsu

A 400-room, four-star ABC Hotel in Hong Kong caters to international business travellers. It opened its doors about twelve years ago and maintained its position well. Although recently new competition has sprung up in its neighbourhood, it is still considered to be a decent hotel for business persons offering good "price-value."

ABC Hotel offers extensive food and beverage facilities, i.e. restaurants, bars, lounges, banquets and meeting rooms etc. Everything in the hotel is run by its own employees, all except the Laundry Department. In its inception stage, the owners and the management had considered the task of running an in-house laundry facilities or contracting the work to an outside cleaner. The owners and the management took a hard stand and finally decided to subcontract the laundry services to an outside agent, Executive Drycleaners.

Executive Drycleaners is a reputable, honest, family-run laundry business. It has been operating within the family for three generations and its product has been professional, the delivery service prompt and the charges very reasonable.

In order to maintain the uniformity of the service, the hotel did not think it was necessary to inform the guests that the laundry service was a subcontract; there was no justification to do so. So the hotel, as is usual, added a small surcharge to the price that Executive Drycleaners charged. For most of the years of operations, there had been no real complaints.

Mr. Malcolm Vaughan, a regular visiting guest from the United

Kingdom, makes his frequent visits to Hong Kong over the past three years and the hotel has always been his place to stay. On one evening, Mr. Vaughan asked that his jacket be dry-cleaned. It was taken to Executive Drycleaners via the Housekeeping Department and upon completion of the dry-cleaning process, it was returned to Mr. Vaughan with the normal dry-cleaning charges added on to his total room charges.

Upon receipt of his jacket, Mr. Vaughan noticed a small dirty spot on it that had not been cleaned. He asked the hotel to remove the spot. The Housekeeping Department obliged and sent the jacket back to Executive Drycleaners with the proper note and identified the spot to be cleaned properly.

Executive Drycleaners returned the jacket with the spot removed. Mr. Vaughan claimed that after the second time it dry-cleaned, the shape of the jacket has been substantially altered, so much so that he could not wear it. He refused to accept it and sent it back to the hotel and promptly checked out returning to the United Kingdom.

To seek compensation for the loss of his jacket, Mr. Vaughan wrote an official letter of complaint to the General Manager of the hotel, John Feng, and asked for compensation of £400. This was the full amount of the value of his jacket when he bought it four years ago. On arrival in the United Kingdom, Mr. Vaughan promptly sent a copy of the purchase receipt for his jacket to prove his ownership and the purchase price.

Since the guest had already left the hotel but leaving behind the letter and his jacket, John Feng notified Executive Drycleaners of the case and asked the company to handle it and communicate directly with Mr. Vaughan in the United Kingdom.

For Executive Drycleaners, this was an unusual case involving a guest of the hotel complaining that the dry-cleaning altered the shape of a jacket. The family management took the extra effort of sending the jacket to an independent garment laboratory for analysis to see if the jacket was really "bent out of shape" via the process of dry-cleaning.

The laboratory test came back negative, indicating there was no visible sign of wear and tear through the dry-cleaning. The laboratory's analysis fee of HK$400 was paid by Executive Drycleaners.

As a compromising gesture while retaining goodwill and business relationship with the hotel, Executive Drycleaners wrote to Mr. Vaughan (c/o John Feng) and offered to make a payment ten times the cost of dry-cleaning the jacket, being HK$500.

To smooth things up, John Feng sent a letter of apology to Mr. Vaughan in the United Kingdom with his jacket properly packaged. As a 15-year hotel veteran, John knows the practice of "The customer is always right" all too well and tried his best to accommodate Mr. Vaughan, especially in this case when dealing with a regular guest of the hotel.

In his personal letter to Mr. Vaughan, John described the process by which Executive Drycleaners examined the wear and tear of the jacket and reiterated their proposed offer to settle this issue by offering him HK$500. Finally, John took great pains to explain that the business relationship between Executive Drycleaners and the hotel was that of the subcontract and not part of the hotel operation. If that was not enough, the hotel would also match the same amount offered by the Executive Drycleaners (i.e. HK$500) to put this matter to rest, making the total amount offered to Mr. Vaughan HK$1,000 or approximately £80.

Privately, John Feng sighed in disgust as he signed his name on the letter: "This is crazy! There's got to be a limit to this 'Customer Is Right' thing … Enough is enough! This is as far as I'll go."

Mr. Vaughan wrote a very nasty letter back claiming that he was insulted by an apparent attempt to compromise his principles. He insisted that the hotel was at fault in handling his personal property, his jacket. When the trust of the guest was given to the hotel to handle the guest's property, any damage caused was the responsibility of the hotel.

Moreover, as far as the outside laboratory test was concerned, he questioned the independence of the whole process since the test was paid for by Executive Drycleaners.

He refused to accept the findings and said that it would be totally irrelevant in this case. Mr. Vaughan stated, "I gave you my jacket to be dry-cleaned. As far as I was concerned, the deal was made between me and you; I really don't care who you gave it to, it's my jacket that was ruined. I refused to accept it and I want compensation for it. I want my full £400 entitlement or I will sue you." His letter was copied to Mr. David Wong, the Executive Director of ABC Hotel group.

The Executive Director, a practising solicitor, turned shrewd businessman, read the letter and scribbled on it: "Bill, take care of this for me!" and passed it along to Bill Foo, his newly hired Vice President of Operations.

Questions for Discussion

1. As the newly hired Vice President of Operations, what would be your action? Analyse your rationale and the possible consequences.
2. Based on your reasoning, draft a letter to Mr. Malcolm Vaughan regarding the matter.

Part II

Housekeeping Management

3

Departmental Meeting

Benny Chan

Queens Hotel has been opened for nearly ten years. The average occupancy remains at 80% since it is located in the Central district. During the monthly staff meeting with the room attendants in the Housekeeping Department, some problems were discovered. The problems could be grouped as follows:

- There was limited choice of food in the staff canteen.
- There were insufficient uniforms for the waiters in the restaurants.
- Everyday, especially after lunch, the linen being circulated was insufficient.
- The new cleaning detergent was not strong enough for cleaning the bathtubs, especially if stains appeared.
- The guest-room supplies (such as ballpoint pens) were not delivered to the floor staff according to the time schedule.
- It was quite difficult to catch the lift when staff were off duty at 16:00.
- It took a long time to get an iron & board from the office for the guests.
- Front desk staff changed room arrangements after the room assignment list was received by floor supervisors.
- Receptionists changed rooms for guests without informing the floor supervisor and released the rooms on their own decision.
- Room service staff did not collect the dirty trays on time after being used by the guest.

- Engineering staff engaged the staff toilet during the day time, and also grouped in the pantry.

Question for Discussion

As the Executive Housekeeper sitting in this meeting, discuss the appropriate actions you will take and the follow-up procedures so as to eliminate these things from happening again.

4

Staff Scheduling

Benny Chan

You are the floor supervisor of Queens Hotel. There will be a group of VIPs arriving at noon tomorrow. You understand that the current staying guests will check out by 9:00 a.m. tomorrow. Since this is a special VIP group, you have to set up sixteen rooms, including complimentary gifts, fruit baskets and flower arrangements for each room and full-bar set-up for a hospitality suite. All you can deploy is four room attendants.

You realize that it takes thirty minutes on average for making up one room, one hour to clean and set up the hospitality suite, and an additional thirty minutes for vacuuming the hallways. Fruit and flower set-up for each room also required an additional five minutes. To make the situation even worse, there will be no clean sheets available before 10:30 a.m. and the complimentary gifts will not be delivered until 11:00 a.m. Finally, you are responsible for final checking of these rooms to ensure that everything is ready.

Question for Discussion

Your job is to plan the schedule in such a way that the deadline can be met if possible. Keep in mind the time limitation, resources available and the problems already known.

5

Manpower Control in Housekeeping Department

Benny Chan

ACE Hotel is located in the business area and has been in operations for four years. It has a 14-storey building plus three basements (see Table 1). As it is near the Mass Transit Railway and the bus stations, a lot of customers enjoyed having meal there. On every Saturday and Sunday, there are local families visiting the hotel to enjoy its facilities. The hotel's most important target are local and Southeast Asian customers. With only 400 guest-rooms (14 suites and 386 normal rooms), the occupancy rate has an average of 90% round the year. The hotel guest-rooms are divided into two types: twin-bedded and double-bedded. All the guest-rooms have no harbour view and are either facing

Table 1:   Hotel Outlets

- Baker Street (coffee shop), located on the ground floor, opening from 6 a.m. till midnight.
- Apple Bar (lobby bar), located on the ground floor, opening from 11 a.m. till 2 a.m. (midnight).
- Rose Restaurant (Chinese restaurant), located on the 1st floor, opening from 11 a.m. till 11 p.m.
- Basement one: the Executive offices.
- Basement two: the staff changing room, Housekeeping Office, Laundry Department and Linen room.
- Basement three: the Engineering Department and the boiler room.
- Guest-rooms, located on 2/F up to 14/F.

the street or other buildings. Since most of the customers are targeted at an economy rate, they are not very concerned about this lack of view.

With economic inflation and the keen competition in the industry, top management is concerned with the money spent on each functional department. Cutting budget and expenses are the exercises that every department head should look at in this current year. One of the largest budget department, the Housekeeping Department, is being informed to cut down the expenses on the personnel part (see Figure 1).

Figure 1:   Budget Expense Categories

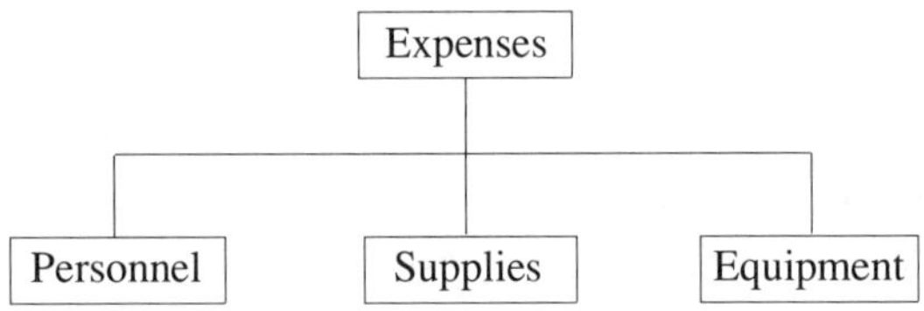

Since the beginning of the hotel operation, the number of room attendants has being been based on the following productivity standard:

1.   16 rooms/one room attendant in Morning Shift (A.M.)
2.   80 rooms/one room attendant in Evening Shift (P.M.)
3.   200 rooms/one room attendant in Overnight Shift (O.N.)

Forty-one room attendants are being employed by the hotel now.

For the floor supervisor part, each one has to take care of two floors. The top floor is mainly suites, with one supervisor being assigned to take care of this floor. There are total thirteen guest floors, therefore seven A.M. floor supervisors, three P.M. floor supervisors, one O.N. supervisor, one public area (P.A.) supervisor and two relievers are employed.

On top of the floor supervisors, there are Andy Chan, the Assistant Housekeeper and Brian Wong, the Assistant Executive Housekeeper (see Figure 2).

Because of the low labour turnover rate in this department, the hotel has the same number of staff in the last four years. The General Manager is now getting Charles Man, the Executive Housekeeper, to cut down

Figure 2: Organizational Chart

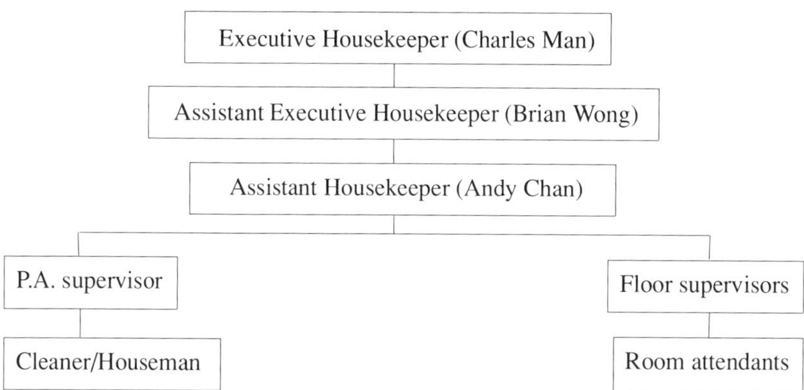

the number of room attendants in the room section since he occasionally found the staff in Housekeeping Department walking around without doing any cleaning work.

The General Manager also invited a consultant to visit the hotel and find out whether there are areas that has to be improved. He also encouraged the department heads to look into the quality control in their own section and empower their subordinates. On the other hand, he stresses on the importance of the operation staff since they are the front-line people facing the customer. The performance of these staff will directly affect the revenue of the hotel. In other words, managers should fully utilize the workforce and praise them so as to get a balance in the workload of the department.

After gathering all the information, Charles started to plan the work for the future so as to cope with the hotel mission. Looking at all the areas, inventory list was the first thing that he has to improve. Then he worked out the cleaning frequency and standard cleaning time, and finally the exact number of staff being required in his department. He discovered that there existed excess labour to meet the current need. Without affecting the morale of the staff, he decided not to employ any new staff should there be any resignation from the present job.

It seems quite logical in doing that. The General Manager and the consultant found that there should be more rooms to improve the existing situation since the turnover rate is not high in the hotel. So, they invited Charles for a meeting to discuss the plan to cut down the number of staff. They asked Charles to work out a possible proposal in cutting down the number of staff without affecting the daily operation and standard of the performance. Charles hesitated whether he could meet their requirements and discussed the idea with his assistant. Both of them started to work out what the management required. The General Manager gave them one week to complete the proposal, otherwise they will be terminated.

Questions for Discussion

1. What should Charles do?
2. Who are the staff Charles is going to lay off?
3. What are the levels of staff to be terminated?
4. What are the areas Charles can also look into so as to eliminate the expenses?

6

Linen Control in Queens Hotel

Benny Chan

The Queens Hotel has existed on the Island for more than twenty-five years. It was a five-star hotel with 600 guest-rooms and located in the heart of business area. The sales mix of the customer was 60% business people and 40% group (tour) visitors. With the huge number of guest-rooms, the hotel employed 900 staff working in different departments. The working environment and atmosphere were very fine and the relationship between workers were very good since they have been working together for a long period.

Half of the members of staff have worked in the hotel for more than twenty years. They seldom have arguments between each other. Most of the department heads or senior staff were promoted from within and most of their experience was gained in this hotel. Spoken communication is the normal means of communication between them and between departments. They "trust" each other and do not have the need to put everything in black and white. There are few complaints between departments or even managerial levels. Everything has gone quite smoothly; everyone has worked quite happily and in harmony in the hotel. The turnover rate in the hotel has been very low when compared with other hotels nearby.

After an annual inspection by headquarters' executives from the United States, they realized that the standard of the hotel was dropping. There is an urgent need to gain more business to the hotel.

After a great deal of consideration, headquarters employed Jack Wilkins as the new General Manager in this hotel. Jack, aged 35, had more than fifteen years' hotel management experience in different countries such as Canada and Thailand. When he reported duty, nothing was changed in the hotel which was running as usual. After that, a special meeting was called and all department heads were invited. During the meeting, he handed out termination letters to all the managers and instructed them to leave their posts once they completely handed over all their duties. He then employed Susan Jones as the Executive Housekeeper, and Ronald Jordan as the Food and Beverage Manager, who had worked with him before in Canada. For the rest of the department heads such as the Front Office Manager and the Purchasing Manager, they would employ locally.

Figure 1:   Organizational Chart of Queens Hotel

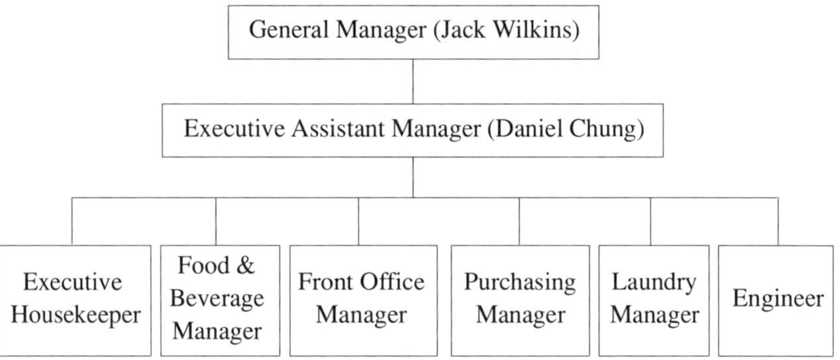

It was a great shock to all the hotel staff and everyone was worried about the security of their jobs. Owing to this sudden change in this hotel, the turnover rate increased more than usual. Some leavers were frightened by the management style and some were even forced by the management to quit the job.

New people looked for change and finally made the hotel run in a more systematic way. A lot of reports or record forms were introduced so as to avoid misunderstanding. This caused a lot of resistance from those staff working there for a long time. Although new staff could fit into the system, there was still a lot of friction which had to be overcome by the managers.

After one year, only 200 staff with more than twenty years' work in the hotel remained in different departments. A total of 140 out of 200 staff were working in the Housekeeping Department as room attendants and supervisors. The existing number of staff working in the Housekeeping Department was 230.

Susan Jones, aged only 25, had five years' working experience as Assistant Housekeeper in a Canadian hotel. She was aggressive and energetic; she always walked around checking on every part daily. As Susan was employed from outsides, there was little support from her subordinates. To make the situation even worse, she employed Peter Chan, an Assistant Executive Housekeeper, from outside instead of by internal promotion.

Peter Chan, aged 27, had worked as Assistant Housekeeper in the King Hotel, a five-star hotel, for five years. He also had an good educational background and graduated from Cornell University. Peter might help Susan in dealing with training and daily operations control in the department. A lot of existing supervisors were disappointed with the decision. According to the tradition of the hotel, Assistant Executive Housekeeper would be internally promoted instead of getting someone externally. As the decision had been made, the supervisors were required to obey what the Executive Housekeeper said.

Figure 2:   Organization of the Housekeeping Department in Queens Hotel

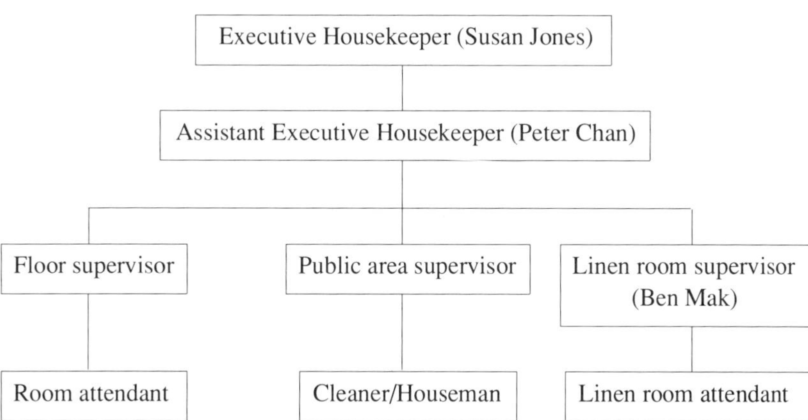

The first thing drawn to Susan and Peter's attention was a shortage of linen supplied in the guest-rooms. Nearly every afternoon, there were not enough wash cloths and bath towels replenished in the guest-rooms. To eliminate the complaints from the Front Office, the room attendant only put the clean towels into those check-out rooms so that the receptionist could send to another new guests. By doing that, complaints arose from those occupied rooms as the guests did not receive enough towels for drying their body. There would be little but not sufficient linen distributed to the floor at around 5 p.m. by the Laundry Department. Linen has distributed evenly between floors and not in accordance with the number of linen required.

A linen inventory count was carried out in the hotel to investigate the problem. After counting all the existing linen in the hotel, there was no problem for the quantity of linen in circulation. With 600 guest-rooms, the number of wash cloths was 4,300 pieces and that of bath towels was 4,500 pieces. Hence each room should have 2 pieces each of bath towels and wash cloths.

During the inventory count, they found out that a lot of new towels had been kept in the storeroom. Besides, some of the towels had been kept in the mini bar cabinet in the floor pantry. These findings gave some help for Susan by knowing the existing number and what she should do in future.

After the inventory count, Susan set up a control system for the linen supply. She requested the floor supervisors to write down the quantities of linen they needed on each day before 9 a.m. (c.f. Table 1). This would help the floor supervisors know the number of rooms needed in cleaning after completing the room report by that time. The linen needed on that day were simply subtracted from the existing linen in the floor pantry against the par level. This gave a clearer picture to the Laundry Department and Linen Room. After collecting all the requisitions, Ben Mak, the Linen Room Supervisor, would draw up a master sheet and give it to the linen room attendant. The linen room attendant would distribute the linen accordingly to each floor after 9 a.m.

Everything seemed to run quite well on the first two days. On the third day, the linen room attendant found out that there was not enough linen distributed to each floor especially after noon. What went wrong?

Table 1:   Linen Requisition Form

Floor: ________________________	Supervisor: ________________	
Item	**Par**	**Request**
Bed sheet	60 pcs.	
Bath towel	60 pcs.	
Hand towel	60 pcs.	
Bath mat	30 pcs.	
Wash cloth	60 pcs.	
Pillow case	60 pcs.	

Were the figures written down by the floor supervisors not accurate or was there a great loss of linen within these two days? Peter Chan was assigned to investigate the problem.

It was 8:10 a.m. Peter was waiting for the service lift. He wanted to patrol all the floors so as to study the linen supply situation in the hotel. He met two floor supervisors in the service lift carrying some cleaned wash cloths. He asked them where they got the cloths. They said they had picked up from the Laundry Department. They also mentioned that those wash cloths were cleaned last evening but needed cooling down before being put into circulation in the Laundry Department. Therefore, Peter went down to the Laundry Department immediately.

What surprised Peter was: nearly all the floor supervisors were in the Laundry Department fetching the cleaned linen they wanted. A lot of cleaned and laundered, but not yet folded, linen was on the floor. Each supervisor got what they needed but without making any record in the Laundry Department. Another surprise was: Jimmy Wan, the Laundry Manager, worked in the hotel for nearly three years; he said this way of work has been running for nearly twenty years. Jimmy also mentioned that this could save a lot of time in folding the linen and cut down the expenses in employing extra people in his department.

Next day, during the supervisors daily briefing, Susan brought up the scene reported by Peter the day before and asked for the supervisors' comments. One of the supervisors said that it was the norm and they had done that for a long time. Some of them mentioned that if they did not go down to the Laundry Department to pick up the cleaned linen in the early morning, their room attendants would blame on them as there was not enough linen for changing. Some supervisors complained about the introduction of the linen requisition form, saying that it would ruin the relationship between the Laundry Department and the Housekeeping Department. Some even challenged the leadership style of the Executive Housekeeper and her assistant.

After a long discussion, both parties compromised on using the linen requisition form for trial for one month. During that period, all the supervisors were permitted to go down to the Laundry Department and Jimmy Wan was then informed.

It was a quiet start to the next day. Every supervisor wrote down the requisition and sent it to the office. No one fetched cleaned linen in the Laundry Department. It was 10 a.m. More than 20 room attendants phased the Housekeeping office saying that they could not continue cleaning the guest-rooms since there were not enough cleaned wash cloths and bath towels. Susan and Peter immediately went down to the Laundry Department to investigate the case. One member of Laundry staff was folding the towels but there were a lot of cleaned towels lying on the floor. Susan spoke to Jimmy to see whether they could spare another member of staff to increase the speed but his reply was negative. Jimmy also complained that sparing one member of staff in folding the towels already affected their routine working schedule. To release the tension, Susan asked one of the linen room attendants to go to the Laundry Department and help them fold the linen.

The story did not come to an end. At 2 p.m., some floors said they did not receive any cleaned linen from the morning onwards. The linen delivery staff was called to the office. He showed all the requisitions to Susan and said that he had just followed their request. As there were no cleaned linen washed by the Laundry Department after 1 p.m., some floors could not receive the linen. Only few floors could receive what they requested on that day. It was already 3 p.m. Some supervisors could not wait for the linen delivery since most of the guest-rooms did not have the wash cloths and bath linen. Instead of going down to the

Laundry Department, they went to other floor pantries "stealing" cleaned linen for use. It was really a hard day to the Executive Housekeeper and her assistant. Besides, there were other complaints from the Assistant Manager and the Front Office receptionists who say some guests could not get enough clean towels in their room.

On the next day, Susan found a note on her desk sent by Jack Wilkins asking her to explain why there were so many guest complaints the previous day about the linen.

Question for Discussion

If you were Susan Jones, how could you handle the situation?

7

Your Towels or Our Tower?

Amos Choy and Simon C. K. Wong

Andy Chow is the Executive Housekeeper of a deluxe five-star hotel, Vinson Hotel, located at Central district. Andy joined this hotel in 1990 as Assistant Executive Housekeeper. He was promoted to the present position on 1 January 1994.

The hotel is owned by a Southeast Asia conglomerate with its headquarters in Singapore. Vinson Hotel has a good reputation based on excellent service, together with new modern decoration and interior design. There are 500 guest-rooms, with 980 employees. The Housekeeping Department employs 193 employees.

The organizational chart of the Housekeeping Department is shown in Figure 1.

With average occupancy rate at 89% annually, the owners were pleased with Vinson Hotel. Andy did some analysis of the nationality and length of stay of the guests, as shown in Table 1.

The revenue generated by the Housekeeping Department in 1995 was HK$15.6 million. Revenue analysis by the Housekeeping Department for the year 1995 is shown in Table 2.

The contractor who takes care of part of the hotel laundry will terminate the contract at 31 August 1996. As an Executive Housekeeper, Andy has to come up with some suggestions to continue providing excellent laundry services to customers.

Andy began his analysis by breaking down the sales revenue of the laundry business (see Table 3).

In addition, the hotel's Laundry Department also takes care of the

Figure 1:   Organizational Chart of Vinson Hotel

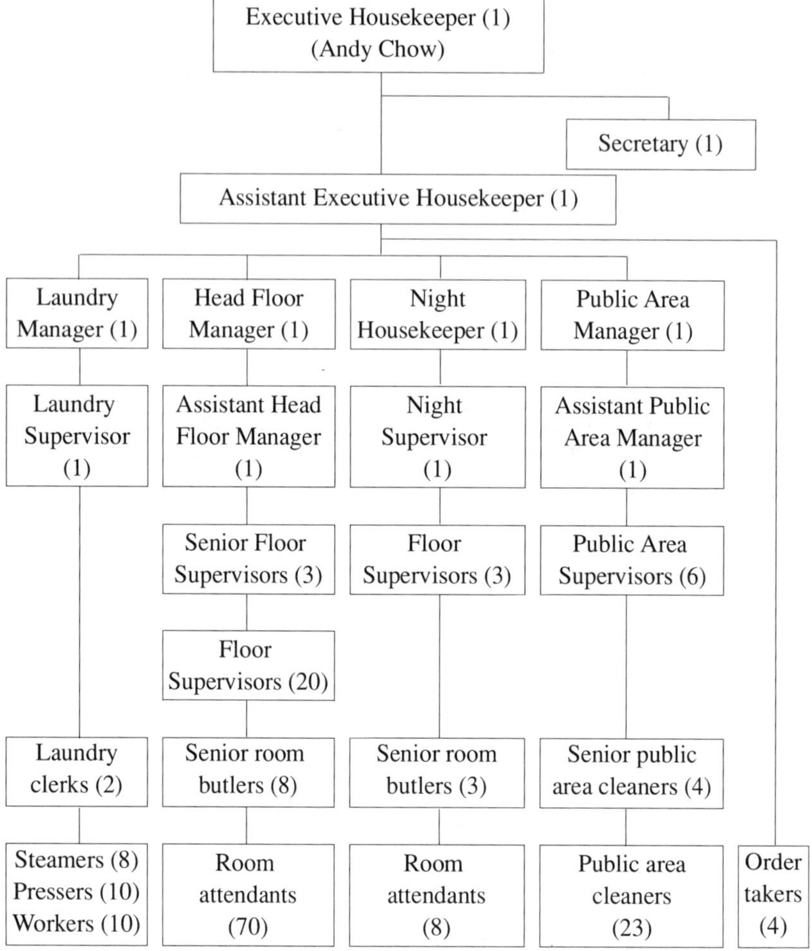

laundry service for staff uniform, guest laundry and part of the linen in guest-rooms, e.g. towels (see Table 4).

At the beginning of 1994, an Environmental Protection Programme was launched throughout the whole hotel and the Housekeeping Department launched an "Environmental Friendly Guest" programme by placing a written statement at every guest washroom. It stated: "For the

Table 1:   Nationality and Length of Stay of Guests in 1995

Guest by nationalities

German	8%
Briton	16%
Japanese	20%
Taiwanese	19%
Mainland Chinese	3%
American	20%
South African	4%
Latin American	5%
Others	5%
Total	100%

Average number of stay per guest (by room nights)

Day use (check out before 11:00 p.m.)	0.5%
1 night	5%
2 nights	30%
3 nights	24.5%
4 nights	17%
5 nights	8%
6 nights	5%
Over 6 nights–14 nights	4%
Over 14 nights	6%
Total	100%

Table 2:   Revenue Analysis of the Housekeeping Department in 1995

Item	% of total revenue
In-room mini bar	23%
Laundry and dry-cleaning	77%
Total	100%

sake of our Earth, please save the cost of washing the towels. If you want to have towels changed, please place at the rattan basket provided. Thank you for your kind contribution to our lovely World."

After this programme was launched, statistics showed a saving of 23% in terms of quantity by pounds. It was also found that guests from the Western world (e.g. American, Canadian and European) did respond positively to this programme.

Table 3:   Breakdown of Laundry Business

Item	% of total revenue
Dry-cleaning	20%
Express cleaning	18%
Normal laundry	48%
Pressing service	14%
Total	100%

Table 4:   Analysis of Internal Laundry Service for the Hotel (in terms of quantity by pounds)

Staff uniform	25%
In-house guest laundry	20%
Guest-room bedsheets, towels	55%
Total	100%

Stephen Hickman, the General Manager, had two ideas in mind to tackle the problem of the additional laundry service after the service by the existing contractor ended:

1. To expand the existing Laundry Department by demolishing the Accounts Office next door to gain additional 2,000 square feet to accommodate equipment and people.
2. To solicit potential outside contractor for performing similar duties.

A floor plan of the existing Laundry Department is shown in Figure 2. Stephen has asked Andy to consider this proposal, calculate the costs, and analyse the pros and cons of this plan.

Stephen also wanted to consider the second proposal. This is to arrange a partial contracting out of the internal laundry services. He wanted Andy to get at least three outside contractors' quotation on how much it would cost to pay for the internal service. The overall purpose of this concept is to try to maximize the manpower and equipment for the profit-earning business, rather than spending time and effort on internal laundry service.

Stephen also asked Andy to give a detailed proposal including all the findings, in one month's time.

Andy immediately searched many commercial laundry companies in Hong Kong. After one week, he selected three laundries which were quite price competitive and with good reputations. In order to make a comprehensive comparison of the three, Andy asked them for their proposals for the new contract.

The following is some of the information from the three proposals:

Proposal from Greenery Laundry

We are the best-equipped laundry in Hong Kong. Our major equipments are all electronically controlled. Applications of chemicals to our washers are made by autofeed system which is also controlled by computers. Our 80,000 square feet premises in Tuen Mun is self-owned. Our Quality Assurance Laboratory, besides closely monitoring our quality, also provides free consultancy services for your selection of linen and uniform. Our distribution team composed of over 20 trucks are prepared to provide delivery services to you at your convenience and even under adverse weather conditions.

Establishments and airlines currently using our service include:

- ten four-star hotels
- three private clubs
- twenty-five airlines
- two chained Chinese restaurants

Quotation for laundry service (1 January 1996 to 31 December 1996) is shown below:

Room linen	**HK$**
Bath robe	6.6
Children bath robe	4.95
Bath mat	1.6
Bath towel	1.65
Bedsheet (all sizes)	3.3
Bidet cloth	1.1
Foot mat	1.27

Figure 2: Floor Plan of the Laundry Department

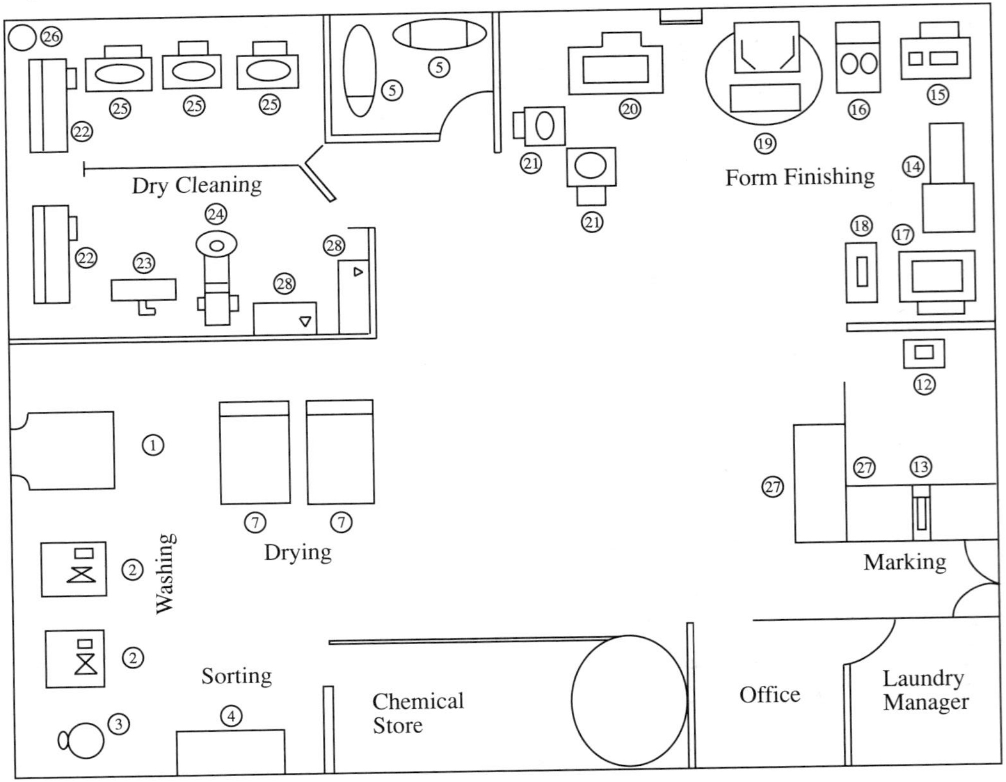

Item	Qty	Equipment	Item	Qty	Equipment
1	1	Wascator FLE-804 Washer Extractor	16	1	Ajax CBS (Boy Size) Double Cabinet Bag Sleever
2	2	Uniwash UW-85-R4 Washer Extractor	17	1	Hoffman Halb-6 Bosom & Body Press
3	1	Wascator C-90M Hydro-Extractor	18	1	Hoffman HNF-3 Shirt Folder
4	1	Stainless Steel Wash Hand Sink	19	1	BMM Weston Durpress 62, Rotary Press
5	2	Shamal 850-500 7.5 H.P. Air Compressor	20	1	Hoffman Halu-53 Legger & Apparel Press
6		Spare Item	21	2	Hoffman Halm-1 & Halm-3 Mushroom Press
7	2	Cissell L44CD42S 50 Kg Dryer	22	2	Spencer 400DR 20 Kg Dry-cleaning Machine
8		Spare Item	23	1	Cissell Model A Vacuum Spotting Board
9		Spare Item	24	1	Cissell FFCD Form Finisher
10		Spare Item	25	3	Hoffman HFC-42SW Utility Press
11		Spare Item	26	1	Cissell 12 bx Vacuum Dryset
12	1	PolyMark Mark IV Marking Machine	27	2	Locally Fabricated Wooden Working Tables
13	1	Texmark Tag-O-Matic Marking Machine	28	2	Locally Fabricated Hand Ironing Tables
14	1	Ajax Cbby (Boy Size) Double Form Body Cabinet	29		Spare Item
15	1	Hoffman Halcy-8 Collar, Cuff & Yoke Press	30		Spare Item

Hand towel	1.21
Face towel	0.77
Lounge towel	2.42
Pillow case	1.43
Baby pillow case	1.1
Top bedsheet	3.3

Food and beverage linen

Cook hat	3.3
Moulton	2.4
Napkin	1.1
Cocktail napkin	0.66
Place mat	1.32
Table cloth (all sizes)	3.85

Proposal from Crystal Laundry

We are a prestigious professional organization in Hong Kong. We have been providing services of laundry and dry-cleaning to various deluxe hotels, restaurants and clubs since 1979. The main laundry plant is located at Wong Chuk Hang, Aberdeen while a subsidiary plant was set at Sha Tin from which we ended up with over 40,000 square feet. We are proud that all the key personnel have been working together for the past fifteen years, thus enabling us to provide laundry service of consistent standard. We also have well-experienced and trained technicians, hence capable of offering a prompt and satisfactory service. In order to ensure the efficient and prompt delivery, we have a transportation team which comprises 18 trucks to cover our entire network of customers at Hong Kong, Kowloon and New Territories.

Current customers include:

- four five-star hotels
- six four-star hotels
- eight private clubs
- two chained restaurants

Quotation for laundry service (1 January 1996 to 31 December 1996) is shown below:

Room linen	**HK$**
Bedsheet (king)	1.94
Bedsheet (single)	1.94
Top sheet	1.94
Pillow case	1.03
Bath towel	1.56
Hand towel	0.87
Face towel	0.52
Bath mat	1.3
Bath robe	4.21
Bidet cloth	0.87
Floor mat	0.87
Duvet cover	16.2
Weighting scale cover	0.87
Food and beverage linen	
Table cloth (large)	3.24
Table cloth (small)	2.37
Cooks' cap	2.05
Cocktail napkin	0.7
Handle protector	0.92
Moulton	2.7
Napkin	0.83
Napkin (Bar)	0.83
Place mat	0.83
Place mat (lace)	0.83
Tray cloth	0.83

Proposal from Cleanest Laundry

Cleanest Laundry is a newly established laundry company owned by the ex-laundry manager of a five-star hotel. It is located in Tsing Yi, New Territories.

Current customers include:

- one five-star hotel
- two three-star hotels
- two private clubs

Quotation from Cleanest (1 January 1996 to 31 December 1996) is shown below:

House linen	**HK$**
Bath towel	1.35
Hand towel	0.8
Face towel	0.55
Bath mat	1.2
Bath robe	4.8
Bath rug	1.3
Bedsheet (all sizes)	1.7
Foot mat	0.95
Pillow case	1
Pillow case inner slip	1
Baby mattress pad	6
Mattress pad (king)	8
Mattress pad (single)	8
Top sheet	1.7
Bath sheet	1.35
Bedside mat	1
Children bath robe	3.8
Baby pillow case	0.65
Quilt cover	8
Weighting scale cover	8
Cooks' cap	1.9
Cocktail napkin	0.7
Napkin	0.75
Place mat	0.75
Lace mat	0.75
Table cloth (below 80 inches × 80 inches)	2.2
Table cloth (over 80 inches × 80 inches)	2.5
Table skirting (per running foot)	2.5
Tray cloth	0.75
Table mat	0.75
Coaster	1
Lounge towel	0.55

As the Vinson Hotel is the flagship of the conglomerate, the bed-sheet are all 100% cotton and the towel are overall heavier than normal deluxe hotel standard. The hotel stocks up a level of five par. Each par is sufficient for hotel operation even using outside laundry service.

To enable him to make a final decision, Andy decided to visit the three laundry plants. He had scheduled two days' visits to all three laundry plants.

Visit to Greenery

On 10 December 1996, Andy arrived at the Greenery Laundry at Tuen Mun at 10:00 a.m. He was warmly welcomed by the General Manager of Greenery, Philip Lau. Philip led Andy to the laundry plant. It was a big plant with 100,000 square feet area.

More than 500 employees were working busily in various production lines. Andy saw many different hotels' towels were being washed and handled together. There were many soil linen lied on the floor. It was quite humid and hot with many steam coming out from the steamer and pressing sections.

Most of the staff are female amahs who mainly came from Mainland China with little knowledge of Cantonese. Male workers are mainly responsible for moving the trucks, containers and the handling of the big machines in the plant.

Philip emphasized that his company was the biggest plant in town plus the highest number of clients in the hotel industry. Philip also proposed that they can offer 15% discount for the hotel executive private laundry service to Vinson Hotel.

Andy felt impressed about the size and smooth operation of Greenery. However, he has a hesitation on the huge production line that mix all linen and towels together. He has a concern on the using of suitable detergents for some many types of linen in Greenery Laundry.

Visit to Cleanest

After staying in Greenery Laundry for two hours, he headed on to visit Cleanest Laundry at Tsing Yi. He arrived at 2:30 p.m. and greeted by its

General Manager, Ivan Li. Ivan led Andy around the laundry plant which is 10,000 square feet, ten times smaller than Greenery. It employs 70 staff.

Andy was impressed with the clean and tidy set-up of the laundry. The air-conditioning was extremely good without the feeling of humid and hot. All employees wear uniform with a name tag carried on it. A platform was built throughout the floor to improve the drainage and avoid slippery. Andy discovered that each container has a clear label on it identifying different company or hotel linen. The employees were trained effectively and handled all marking, dry-cleaning and machine operation. Besides, a special line of truck delivery was developed to go to different client for collection and delivery service.

Ivan explained to Andy that Cleanest Laundry was newly set up. Although the plant is small in size, it can provide 100% attention to the client's linen. This is the reason why they develop a labelled container and schedule a time for each client in the production line (for example, Client A from 10:00 a.m.–12:00 noon, Client B from 12:00 noon– 2:00 p.m.) to avoid the mixing of wrong linen together.

Ivan further said that they had developed a mini laundry internally in the plant to handle emergency or express service that suddenly requested with only 20% service charge added on top. Ivan also emphasized that he believed in training and would arrange at least two hours' training per month to each employee. At the moment, it has 70 employees in the plant. Andy felt satisfied with Ivan's new approach in management; nevertheless, he would like to see the third laundry tomorrow before making a comparison.

Visit to Crystal

Andy visited Crystal Laundry on 11 December 1996. He arrived at Aberdeen at 11:00 a.m. and met Freeman Cheung, the General Manager. Crystal Laundry has 40,000 square feet with 250 employees. Uniform was provided but quite dirty; most male employees even did not wear any T-shirt. This may be due to the hot and humid temperature in the plant.

Freeman Cheung was proud of his efficient production team. The plant can handle different clients, for example, hotel, Chinese restaurant, commercial firms and clubs. However, the containers only attach a movable label on top. This may due to the multi-usage of containers for different client.

Freeman agreed that he can provide emergency service to Vinson Hotel with the advantage of having the plant situated in the same Hong Kong Island. However, when Andy asked about the routing and scheduling of the truck delivery service, Freeman just said a flexible routing applied in the daily work. Freeman said he can direct the trucks to move to any clients that require extra service or under urgency situation.

Andy spent two hours in Crystal Laundry and Freeman once again offered a very attractive offer by having 10% discount if Vinson Hotel signed the contract with him for a minimum of two years. Andy was impressed; however, he insisted to go back to the hotel for reporting this offer. Andy promised to reply to Freeman in two weeks' time. Andy left Crystal Laundry at 4:15 p.m.

A Comparison of the Three Laundry

Andy, after visiting all three Laundry plants, decided to make a comparison in order to help him see the pros and cons of the three. His summary of observation is given in Table 5.

Additional comments are given as follows:

1. Greenery is the biggest and most established of the three laundries. They are very experienced in processing hotel laundry and have the capacity to handle any increase in volume. However, owing to the volume that they handle, they may not be able to provide any special attention to our linen or any special requirements that we may have. Also, their prices are the highest of the three laundries.

2. Crystal has the advantage of being nearby; it is located in Aberdeen. It is also big and well-established. However, the general observation of their processed linen is that they are not of a standard that we require.

Table 5:   A Comparison of the Three Laundry

	Greenery	Crystal	Cleanest
Size	100,000 sq. ft.	40,000 sq. ft.	10,000 sq. ft.
Address	Tuen Mun 45 mins/trip	Aberdeen 15 mins/trip	Tsing Yi 45 mins/trip
Operating hours	08:00–17:00 17:00–22:00	08:00–17:00 extendible	08:00–17:00 extendible
Staffing	500	250	70
Equipment	Full range with tunnel washer	Full range	Full range
Cleanliness	Good (humid)	Fair (humid)	Good with air- conditioning
Soil linen handling	Very good	Average	Average
Lift	3	1	4
Loading dock	Good	Good	Good
Delivery container	Plenty (Stub nail found)	Plenty (Stub nail found)	Good finishing
Chemical	Economic brand	Economic brand	Deluxe brand
Transport action	25 trucks	15 trucks	6 trucks

3. Cleanest was only set up in October 1995. Their equipment
    is new and modern. They started to service the ABC Hotel
    (a five-star hotel) about a month ago and the comments from
    the client are good. Although they are new and do not have
    the experience yet, they do appear to place great emphasis on
    quality products.

Table 6 shows the quantity of linen that normally sent to contractor
at a 100% occupancy situation.

Questions for Discussion

1. In your opinion as a General Manager, would you consider to
    demolish the Accounts Office and expand the existing Laundry
    Department in order to cope with the needs? Justify your answers.

Table 6:   Quantity of Linen Normally Sent to Contractor

Items	Quantity
Bedsheet (king)	24,685
Bedsheet (single)	31,375
Top sheet	30
Pillow case	44,246
Bath towel	28,785
Hand towel	187
Face towel	346
Bath mat	12,597
Bath robe	9,904
Bidet cloth	840
Duvet cover	9
Foot mat	17,922
Children bath robe	2
Food and beverage linen	
Table cloth (large)	41
Table cloth (small)	6,428
Cooks' cap	77
Cocktail napkin	14
Moulton	15
Napkin	41,002
Place mat	1,132
Tray cloth	76

2.   If you are the Executive Housekeeper, what criteria you would like to set for selecting a suitable contractor?

3.   Assuming you are Andy Chow, which contractor would you select? Give reasons based on the facts provided in this case.

Part III

Food and Beverage Management

8

Filling Up the Ballroom!

Simon C. K. Wong

Excellent Hotel is a five-star hotel located in Central district. It has 450 rooms managed by 800 staff. The Food and Beverage Department employs 350 staff with six outlets, including a coffee shop, a discothèque, a French grill room, a ballroom, a Chinese restaurant and a lobby bar. The ballroom can accommodate a maximum of 250 guests at 25 tables.

Excellent Hotel has a good occupancy rate averaging 83% annually. Most of the customers are bankers, lawyers, government officials and presidents of various big corporations. Average room rate per night is HK$2,850 in 1995. Since the hotel targets for business travellers, its business facilities include:

- a business centre with full service provided,
- a health centre with an indoor swimming pool and gymnasium,
- a hairdressing salon,
- a lobby souvenir shop,
- in-house laundry service,
- a tour desk,
- an Executive Deluxe floor with speedy check-in and check-out, complimentary buffet breakfast (7:00 a.m.–10:30 a.m.) and pre-dinner cocktail (5:00 p.m.–7:00 p.m.),
- limousine service between hotel and airport.

The business for Food and Beverage Department is good especially during lunch hours. All outlets are full because of the demand for quality food and service in Central district. However, the business on Saturdays, Sundays and Public Holidays drops due to the lack of customers who are mainly office workers in the district.

Overall, the business generated by various outlets is satisfactory. However, the revenue generated by the ballroom fluctuates depending on the season. The ballroom is decorated with deluxe interior design, elegant set-up and high adaptability. It is a rectangular-shaped ballroom without any pillars. The stage is well equipped with all high-technology audio-visual equipment.

In the previous year, the ballroom gained substantial business for conferences, meetings, and annual dinners for big corporations. However, for private functions like weddings and birthday parties, business was not satisfactory. The Marketing Research Manager, Samson Cheng, presented his statistics to the Food and Beverage Manager, Victor Shum. Tables 1 and 2 were his findings for 1995.

Excellent Hotel had developed different packages for different market segments:

1. ***Business Lunch and Meeting***
    a. **Executive Package 1**
       One coffee break sit snack
       From: 9:00 a.m.–1:00 p.m. or
                2:00 p.m.–5:00 p.m.
       A minimum number of persons: 20
       Per person: HK$350 per session

    b. **Executive Package 2**
       One coffee break with snack and
       Buffet lunch at the coffee shop/function room
       From: 9:00 a.m.–1:00 p.m. or
                2:00 p.m.–5:00 p.m.
       Per person: HK$450 per session

2. ***Conference and Meeting Package***
    a. **Meeting Planner 1**
       One coffee break with assorted pastries and
       Set lunch at the coffee shop/function room

Table 1: Breakdown of Business Income in 1995

Type of business	% of total revenue	Average revenue per customer
Business lunch & meeting	20	HK$400
Conference dinner	18	700
Seminar lunch & meeting	20	350
Annual dinner, Spring dinner	12	750
Wedding	14	580
Cocktail reception	13	300
Others	3	280
Total	100	620

Table 2: The Utilization of the Ballroom by Months, 1995

Month	Occupancy rate (no. of days per month)
January	25%
February	55%
March	65%
April	65%
May	75%
June	40%
July	20%
August	20%
September	25%
October	55%
November	75%
December	97%
Average per year	51.42%

From: 9:00 a.m.–1:00 p.m. or
2:00 p.m.–5:00 p.m.
Per person: HK$500 per session

b. **Meeting Planner 2**

Two coffee breaks with assorted pastries, dim sum and
sandwiches
Chinese/Western buffet lunch at function room of outlets

From: 9:00 a.m.–5:00 p.m.

Per person: HK$750

  c. **Meeting Planner 3**

Two coffee breaks with assorted pastries, dim sum and sandwiches

Western set lunch and dinner at French grill room or Chinese lunch and dinner at Chinese restaurant

From: 9:00 a.m.–5:00 p.m.

Per person: HK$1,000

All Meeting Packages include the following accessories:
- Overhead projector with screen,
- Flip chart, Whyteboard with coloured markers,
- Stationery and writing materials,
- Refreshments and candies,
- Distilled water.

All price subject to 10% service charges.

3. *Wedding Packages*

  a. **Romance Package 1**

Price: HK$5,500 per table of 10 persons

Chinese banquet plus:
- Four-tier dummy wedding cake,
- "Romance" non-alcoholic cocktails for every guest,
- Wedding march with dry ice presentation with music,
- Free invitation cards,
- Complimentary parking for five cars on that night,
- Honeymoon Suite for the night with a bottle of champagne,
- Flower bouquet for the bride,
- American breakfast for the bride and groom in their room or at coffee shop,
- Complimentary limousine service for two hours by Mercedes-Benz car.

  b. **Honey and Romance Package 2**

Price: HK$7,500 per table of 10 persons

Chinese banquet plus:
- Five-tier dummy wedding cake,

- "Love and Romance" non-alcoholic cocktails for every guest,
- Wedding march with dry ice presentation with music,
- Free invitation cards,
- Complimentary parking for ten cars on that night,
- Honeymoon Harbour View Suite for the night with a bottle of champagne,
- Rose flower bouquet for the bride,
- American breakfast for the bride and groom in their room or at coffee shop,
- Complimentary limousine service for four hours by Mercedes-Benz car,
- Free banquet banner,
- One standard room of hotel for day use for the relatives (2:00 p.m.–12:00 midnight) on that day.

c. **Optional Added-value Package**

Excellent Hotel has linked with several reputable companies which offer discount for clients who take advantage of the wedding package:

- Bride and groom photography,
- Video tape recording and editing service,
- Extra car rental service,
- Honeymoon Travel Plan — to stay in our chained hotel abroad with discount,
- Design of wedding invitation card,
- Rental of bride and groom dress service (including Chinese gown).

d. **Beverage Package**

Excellent Hotel also offers various Beverage Packages for Wedding clients.

- *Beverage Package 1*

  All types of soft drinks and beer from 7:00 p.m.–11:00 p.m., unlimited supply (HK$900 per table).

- *Beverage Package 2*

  All types of soft drinks, beer plus orange juice from 7:00 p.m.–11:00 p.m., unlimited supply (HK$1,300 per table).

- *Beverage Package 3*
  An open bar with orange juice, spirits and other alcoholic drinks from 5:00 p.m.–8:00 p.m. (HK$200 per person).
- *Beverage Package 4*
  An open bar with orange juice, spirits and other alcoholic drinks from 6:00 p.m.–11:00 p.m. (HK$400 per person).

After the opening of the Convention and Exhibition Centre in Wan Chai, Excellent Hotel lost much of its corporate convention and meeting business. In addition, the wedding business was difficult to boost because of the severe competition by other hotels in Hong Kong, which were offering attractive rates and wedding packages for this niche market. In addition, the location of the hotel is not too appealing for wedding couples.

The General Manager, Davidson Jones, asked the Marketing Department and the Food and Beverage Department to devise a marketing strategy and action plan to boost the occupancy rate of the function room. The analysis shows occupancy rate to be as low as 20% during the Summer period, and the hotel owner has indicated that the proposal should particularly highlight this period.

In this connection, an *ad hoc* committee headed by the Resident Manager was formed with the following six members:

• Food and Beverage Manager	Victor Shum
• Banquet Sales Manager	Eliza Hung
• Banquet Service Manager	Thomas Tam
• Director of Sales	Mary Kwan
• Marketing Research Manager	Samson Cheng
• Resident Manager	Patrick Waldrof

A brainstorming session was held on 26 March 1996. The objective of this meeting was to try to generate a range of alternatives for increasing the ballroom sales.

During the meeting, different categories of topics were generated without any pre-judgemental bias. Some interesting ideas came out, as shown below:

- Who is/may be our customers?

- Why our customers choose us?
- Push or pull marketing?
- Package marketing — Conference plus dinner and cocktails.
- Any new market?
- Product development — Is the ballroom concept too outdated?
- Why has the hotel experienced poor business during Summer time?
- Product change — Can the ballroom change to another product during Summer time to attract different business?
- What is the general image of the hotel?
- What positioning is our ballroom compared to similar facilities in other hotels?

Questions for Discussion

1. If you are the General Manager, what marketing strategy would you apply in relation to this product, i.e. the ballroom?
2. If you are the Director of Sales, in which market positioning would you place the ballroom?
3. If you are the Food and Beverage Manager, what would you do to boost the sales of the ballroom during Summer time?

9

The Closing Down of the Starlet Grill

Vickie Siu and Simon C. K. Wong

Owned by a local conglomerate, the Outrigger Hotel is a medium tariff hotel located at Tsim Sha Tsui East. The hotel was opened in 1983 and has 450 guest-rooms. At present, it employs 750 staff.

Recently, Peter Lee, the Food and Beverage Manager, has been delegated by management a very tough job. Peter has just finished attending an important meeting with the owner and the hotel's Executive Committee which comprised the General Manager Samson Wallace, the Resident Manager Donald Maclalin, and the Financial Controller James Fung. The Personnel Manager, Elizabeth Chow, was also in the meeting.

A major decision was made during the meeting on 28 March 1996. The owner decided to close down one of the food and beverage outlets in the hotel, the Starlet Grill, in six months' time. The reason is simply the poor revenue the outlet has generated in the past two years. The target date to close down the Starlet Grill is 30 September 1996. According to the existing floor plan of the Grill, the vacated area could be rented out to ten retail shops.

As Food and Beverage Manager, Peter oversees four restaurant outlets, room service, three kitchens and steward. Besides Starlet Grill, the hotel has a lobby lounge, a coffee shop located in the hotel lobby, and a Chinese restaurant on the fourth floor. While the lounge, the coffee shop and room service share the same main kitchen, the Starlet Grill and the Chinese restaurant each has a separate kitchen.

The following organizational chart illustrates the structure of the Food and Beverage Department (with a total of 279 employees):

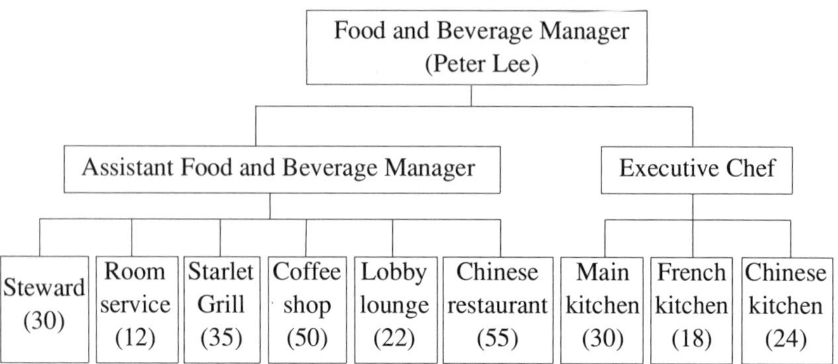

Having a seating capacity of 80, the Starlet Grill has been one of the top French grill rooms in Hong Kong in the 1980s and was famous for its deluxe decoration and excellent food quality. To provide a French-style personal service, the outlet maintained a staff to guest ratio at around 1 to 2. Most of the patrons of the restaurant were Westerners who were the regular visitors of the hotel.

In recent years, however, the hotel has encountered a dramatic shift of its clientele base from European and North American to Southeast Asian such as Taiwanese and Indonesian. In most cases, this new group of clientele prefer to dine at the coffee shop and the bar since they can get faster service at lower prices. As a result, the business level of the Grill is far less than satisfactory in the 1990s. Table 1 illustrates the financial background of the Grill over the past five years.

Overall, the financial status of the Grill has deteriorated. To rectify the situation, Peter discontinued the employment of part-timers at the Grill in 1995. Still, the average monthly net profit has dropped to around HK$12,259. Comparatively speaking, the revenue generated from renting out the space of the Grill is anticipated to be HK$4,800,000 per year (10 retail shops × HK$40,000 monthly rental × 12 months).

Well before the decision concerning closing down the Grill was made, Peter made attempts to bring down the food cost. However, the

Table 1: Financial Background of the Starlet Grill, 1991 to 1995 (in Hong Kong dollars)

	1991	1992	1993	1994	1995
Sales revenue	$9,720,000	$10,750,000	$10,920,000	$10,976,000	$10,750,000
Average restaurant occupancy	85%	80%	75%	70%	60%
Average check	$500	$600	$650	$700	$800
Cost					
Full-time labour	$2,916,000	$3,265,920	$3,690,489	$4,059,540	$4,465,500
Part-time labour	336,000	540,000	600,000	450,000	0
Food	2,850,000	3,332,500	3,385,200	3,410,400	3,333,120
Beverage	1,458,000	1,728,000	1,801,800	1,646,400	1,827,840
Overhead	874,800	978,250	1,015,560	1,026,256	978,432
Net profit	1,285,200	905,330	426,951	383,404	147,108

Executive Chef was most worried about the impact this may bring to the food quality and thus insisted that the food cost should be maintained at over 30%. The Chef's concern originated from the guest complaints about the shrank food portion.

At the same time, there were staff morale problems in the Grill which was a result of the low business level and thus less income from tips. On one occasion, seven staff called in sick on different days in the same week and there were rumours that they took the day off to attend job interviews. Even if they are at work, they are reluctant to receive orders from the Grill Manager. The service quality received the worst comments ever through the guest commentary system. Apart from these, three waiters of the Starlet Grill took the liberty of requesting transfer to other food and beverage outlets without having the consent of the Grill Manager and acknowledging the Personnel Manager. This resulted in tremendous confusion among outlet managers and nearly caused internal competition for staff within the Food and Beverage Department.

Before the proper announcement from the General Manager, there were already rumours all over the Food and Beverage Department that the company would close down one outlet and more in the future. The rumours led to several staff resignations. On 13 April 1996, three waiters of the Starlet Grill, Danny Cheung, Jimmy Wong and Warren Chiu, tendered their resignations. Both Danny and Jimmy were newly hired still within their probation periods while Warren had served the outlet for more than two years.

Four days afterwards, four cooks of the French kitchen, Victor Leung, Steve Ko, Wilson Chan and Paul Leung, also tendered their resignations. Among them, Steve had served the hotel since its opening while Paul had just received the "Employee of the Month" award in March. On 20 April, three steward amahs, two captains of the Starlet Grill and two waiters of the coffee shop as well resigned from their positions. Peter also heard from the Personnel Manager that a number of staff of other departments were looking for jobs in other hotels or catering institutes.

On 23 April 1996, Peter received a letter from the Hong Kong Union of Cooks. In the letter, the union leader Lee Ming-sum wrote: "On behalf of your company cooks, we demand the employer gives full redundancy compensation if your company decides to close down an outlet. We would be grateful if the employer could discuss the detailed compensation package with us at your earliest convenience."

Samson Wallace, the General Manager, was very concerned about the current staff movements as rumours also spread externally. Lately, he has received many calls and letters from guests asking if it was true that the hotel would close down the Starlet Grill. Many regular Western customers wrote to him expressing their concern and urged him to retain this restaurant. They said that the decision was most disappointing and they might patronize other hotels should that decision materialize.

An urgent meeting was called upon on 26 April 1996 to discuss remedial measures and strategies. The meeting comprised the owner, the General Manager, the Resident Manager, the Food and Beverage

Manager, the Financial Controller, the Personnel Manager and the Public Relations Manager.

After the meeting, the owner insisted on carrying out the original decision for the sake of a more attractive and steady income generated by shop rentals. Despite this decision, he preferred to retain most of the staff who worked for the Grill and the French kitchen. It is the desire of the hotel to maintain its reputation rather than to join in the redundancy trend. Nevertheless, several major guidelines were given during the meeting:

1. To reduce rumours about the Starlet Grill restaurant;
2. To maintain staff morale;
3. To minimize the negative impact of closing down the Starlet Grill by keeping each employee in the restaurant and kitchen as long as he or she wishes to stay;
4. To arrange transfer or relocation of employees as much as possible;
5. To let staff leave by natural resignation rather than to make them redundant;
6. To prepare an action plan for the six months before the closing down of the Grill to ensure a smooth transition;
7. To inform staff concerned positively about this decision.

Peter was asked to propose detailed action plan. All members in the Executive Committee will assist him to fulfil the objectives and complete the tasks. The proposal will have to reach the General Manager's office in four day's time, i.e. on 30 April.

Questions for Discussion

1. Calculate the following (in terms of %) for each of the past five years and evaluate whether it is sensible to close down the Starlet Grill.
   a. Labour cost (full-time and part-time)
   b. Food cost
   c. Beverage cost

    d. Overhead cost

    e. Net profit

2. Identify the present operational problems of the Starlet Grill and discuss how Peter Lee should handle them in the next six months.

3. Design an action plan detailing out the critical path for the next six months leading to the closing down of the Starlet Grill.

Part IV

Front Office Management

10

The Rooms Division Budget

Rosalie Wong

The Nara Hotel is a high tariff hotel located in Causeway Bay. It has 300 guest-rooms, two function rooms and one of the largest ballrooms among hotels in the vicinity. The hotel is wholly owned by a local company.

The Nara Hotel has started business for nearly one year and its target customers are business travellers and convention delegates. Because of its good location, the occupancy of the hotel has averaged 90% monthly. The owner and the top management are quite pleased with the good performance.

Unfortunately, with one newly opened hotel and the renovation of two hotels in the close proximity, fierce competition seems to be emerging. In order to extend the market share, retain the customers and secure more return business, the management team of the Nara Hotel is required to consider alternatives in upgrading their guest services. You have recently been appointed as the Rooms Division Manager of the Nara Hotel and therefore you are invited to attend the management team meeting.

During the meeting, the General Manager comments that upgrading the guest-room supplies are necessary in order to gain competitive advantages against other hotels. He recommends that more amenities should be provided for each in-house guest, such as good-night chocolate and daily fruit. However, he emphasizes that this new campaign should be incorporated into the existing departmental budget (see Table 1) so as to maintain the targeted return on investment.

Table 1: Rooms Division Budget (Profit & Loss Account)

	$ thousand	%
Sales		
Foreign independent traveller	4,800	3.4
Commercial	19,000	13.6
Foreign independent traveller discounted	14,800	10.6
Travel agent special	24,000	17.1
Convention delegates	76,600	54.7
Airlines special	900	0.6
Others	0	0
Total Sales	140,100	100
Departmental expenses		
Full-time staff		
Payroll (P)	20,500	14.6
Staff-related expenses (R)	2,200	1.6
P&R expenses	22,700	16.2
Less: 10% service charges	14,010	10.0
Net P&R expenses	8,690	6.2
Other expenses		
Casual labour	270	0.2
Cleaning supplies	420	0.3
Complimentary food and drink	1,120	0.8
Contract cleaning	800	0.6
Decoration	600	0.4
Guest supplies	3,200	2.3
Laundry	1,300	0.9
Linen	420	0.3
Music & entertainment	15	0
Printing & stationery	280	0.2
Reservation expenses	280	0.2
Rooms commission	1,100	0.8
Telephone, telex, fax & postage	130	0.1
Transportation and travel	10	0
Uniform	150	0.1
Miscellaneous	10	0
Total other expenses	10,105	7.2
Total expenses	18,795	13.4
Departmental profit	121,305	86.6

Supplementary Notes

- On average, 50% of the occupancy is double occupancy.
- Cost for one good-night chocolate is HK$2.5.
- Cost for one fruit portion is HK$3.5.

Question for Discussion

You are being asked to submit a proposal on upgrading the guest-room supplies. What are your suggestions?

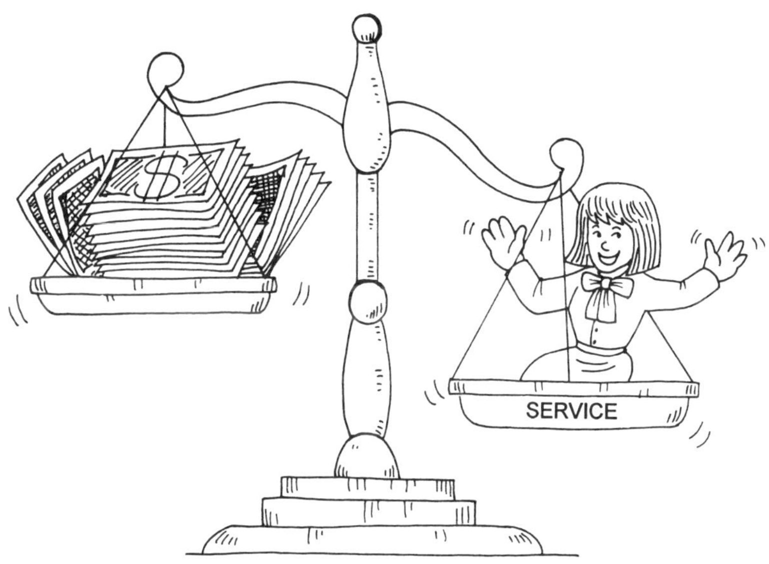

11

Who Is the Best?

Rosalie Wong

The Sparks Mirage Hotel in Wan Chai was built in 1980 by Mirage Hotels Ltd., an U.K.-based company. Recently, the hotel was acquired by a local hotels group, The Chester Group.

The hotel was renamed as The Chester Sparks Hotel after the acquisition. It has been redecorated to project a new image conveying comfort and efficiency. The front office is also decorated and furnished to conform with this image, and its computer system has been upgraded. A job sharing scheme is going to be implemented.

However, according to the records, there has been a rapid turnover of front office staff in the past six months. Two receptionists and one experienced, long-serving supervisor has left and the remaining supervisor has been at the hotel for only seven months, starting as a receptionist. Other front office receptionists of the hotel are all rather young, although they are willing to learn. Sometimes they really need a "firm hand" regarding their appearance and giggling.

You, as a Front Office Manager, are dealing with the applicants for the position of a receptionist. Who is the best?

The following are your applicants and their summarized personal details on the application forms:

Alex Lo	22 years old. Alex has previous hotel concierge experience. He was not employed for nine months until he found his present job. Now, he works as a sales executive for an insurance company.

Daniel Tang   27 years old. Married with two children. Now, he works as an overnight receptionist at Noosa Hotel. He did not complete the question on his health record on the application form.

Vivian Chan   21 years old. She is a diploma holder and was graduated from a hotel school last year. No success in obtaining employment after graduation. She was trained in the front desk at Sea World Resort during the placement period.

Gary Liu   25 years old. Married with two children. He enjoys working in the hotel industry and works as a restaurant cashier at The Beach Hotel. He joined the hotel for four years and started at the same position.

Judy Wong   26 years old. Widow with one child. She has been a housewife after married. She joined The Plaza Hotel as a telephone operator since the beginning of last year.

Wendy Au   23 years old. Health report states that she had a car accident one year before and now she is still receiving treatment. She joined The Tower Hotel for two years starting as a front office cashier. Now she works in the mail and information desk.

12

The Loss Case

Rosalie Wong

The Hotel

The 350-room Grand Palace Hotel is a five-star hotel located in Central. It is designed as a city hotel primarily for the growing business and conventions market. The Grand Palace Hotel was built in 1991. The property is 80% owned by Palace Hotels & Resorts (the Canadian-based hotel group) and 20% by Canadian Airlines. The hotel is presently managed by a local hotel management company.

In order to provide maximum security for in-house guests, the Marlock (ML) key system has been installed in the hotel. The advantage of the ML system is that it can meet the special access control of both front- and back-of-the-house areas. It controls and documents all activities from a central computer. Moreover, it can give the access information of each guest-room in detailed printouts. This enables the hotel to maintain a minute-by-minute audit trail showing the date, time, and individual who entered or attempted to enter every door on the property. The system can also identify the name of any hotel staff by their own keys. When the room is entered by an employee, it prints out the individual's name rather than just a code number.

The hotel includes four food and beverage outlets, a business centre, a health centre and a 50-metre outdoor swimming pool which is located on the 12th floor. There are two accesses to the pool from the floor. For security reasons, closed circuit television (CCTV) is installed at the entrance of each access door. Moreover, a security officer is stationed at the two accesses daily from 8:00 a.m. to 8:00 p.m. For the rest of the time, the door is kept locked by the security department and it will be double-checked by an assistant manager daily.

The Assistant Manager Team

An assistant manager of the Grand Palace is responsible for the overall operation, mainly front office departments, of the hotel. The assistant manager team consists of one Senior Assistant Manager, four Assistant Managers and five Guest Services Officers (see Figure 1).

Besides the floor operation, the Senior Assistant Manager is also responsible for conducting training courses for new assistant managers and "refresher" courses for existing staff. Although training courses are conducted, no written training materials exist for the assistant manager desk. Since the existing Senior Assistant Manager has been in the position for more than three years, he can provide a very comprehensive training programme for staff without using written training documents.

Recently, the experienced Senior Assistant Manager resigned. On the one hand, the vacancy cannot be filled by existing assistant managers as they are not ready to fill up the position. On the other hand, to ensure a full team at the assistant manager desk, Jackie Lai has been promoted to the team.

Figure 1:   Organizational Chart of the Assistant Manager Team

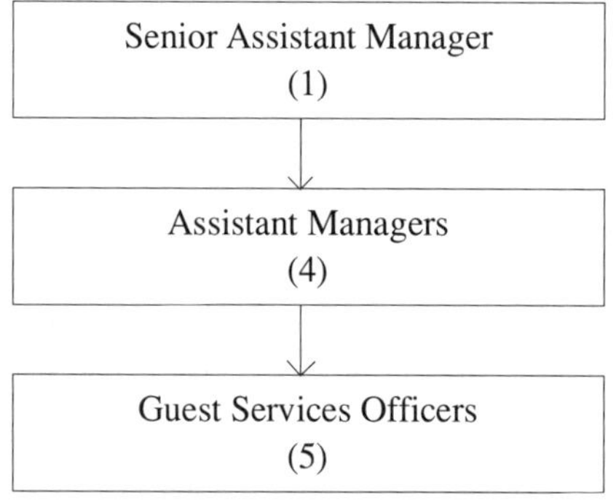

Jackie was formerly the chief receptionist of the hotel and he was responsible for the overall operations of the front office. Jackie has over five years' front office experience gained in two hotels. He started as a front office receptionist. In the last three years, he has been working at the Grand Palace Hotel. Owing to Jackie's loyalty to the hotel and his relevant working experience, he was selected for the promotion even his academic qualifications are limited to matriculation.

Limited training and guidance were provided to Jackie at the time he was promoted since there was nobody capable of conducting the training. Moreover, Jackie was promoted internally; he was thought to have a thorough knowledge about the hotel and the daily operations of the front office.

The Incident

One week after Jackie's promotion, he faced a challenge. On 14 January at around 12:25 p.m., Mr. Klaus Goodman of Room 1226 approached the front desk and reported that his laptop computer was missing from his room. Mr. Goodman had come to Hong Kong and stayed in the Grand Palace Hotel with five other colleagues; they were with the Australian Insurance Group.

At that time, Jackie was with some other guests in the lobby. When he was informed by the front desk clerk about Mr. Goodman's case, Jackie immediately accompanied Mr. Goodman back to Room 1226 and conducted an investigation but to no avail. Since Mr. Goodman was rather concerned about the loss, he decided to report it to the police.

Jackie tried to assist Mr. Goodman by all means in order to create goodwill. Jackie thought that it would be much easier for Mr. Goodman to report the incident to the police if he had all details on hand. Jackie thus compiled the Guest Property Lost Report (see Table 1) and provided a copy of the report to Mr. Goodman. Moreover, arrangement was made to have a bellboy accompany Mr. Goodman to the nearest police station.

To log down all details relating to the incident, Jackie wrote the following report about Mr. Goodman's case in the assistant manager log book.

Table 1:   Guest Property Lost Report (Internal Use Only)

Reported at <u>1225</u> hrs   on <u>14/01/1996</u>

Guest Name: <u>Mr. Klaus Goodman</u>   Room No.: <u>1226</u>

Arrival Date: <u>11/01/1996</u>   Departure Date: 16/01/1996

Address: <u>164 Frank Street, Southport, Queensland 4215, AUSTRALIA</u>

Passport No.: <u>B2763591</u>   Nationality: <u>Australia</u>

Date / Time of discovery of loss: <u>14/01/1996</u>   at   <u>approximately 1140 hrs</u>

Location: <u>Room 1226</u>

Description of Property Involved	**Cost When Purchased**
one Toshiba notebook computer	approx. HK$25,300
one Sharp digital diary	approx. HK$ 2,370
one Hewlett-Packard printer (bubble jet)	approx. HK$ 1,380
plus several sets of wires, cables, and the	
blue cover bag	
	Total approx. HK$29,050

Where / how was the property kept?

<u>The above lost items were placed inside a blue cover bag, positioned next to Mr.
Goodman's brief case and leaning against the leg underneath the writing desk.</u>

Property was last seen at <u>0930</u> hrs   on   <u>14/01/1996</u>   by   <u>Mr. Goodman</u>

Is guest travelling with a group?   Yes / No̶

If so, identify group   <u>The Australian Insurance Group</u>

Jackie
____
Assistant Manager's Signature

p. p. Jackie
____
Security Officer's Signature

On 14 January, Mr. Klaus Goodman of Room 1226 approached the assistant manager and claimed that some of his belongings were found to be missing from his room.

After the investigation, the following items were found to be missing from Room 1226:

- one Toshiba notebook computer   approx. HK$25,300
- one Sharp digital diary   approx. HK$ 2,370
- one Hewlett-Packard printer (bubble jet)   approx. HK$ 1,380
- plus several sets of wires, cables, and the blue cover bag

The total value is approximately HK$29,050.

Mr. Goodman left his room at approximately 9:30 a.m. and went to meet with his colleagues — the Australian Insurance Group. At that time, the aforementioned items were still inside the room placed inside a blue cover bag, positioned next to Mr. Goodman's brief case and leaning against the leg underneath the writing desk.

Mr. Goodman returned to his room at approximately 11:15 a.m. to retrieve a name card but was not sure whether the said items were still inside the room as he did not look.

After meeting with Mr. John Smith (Room 1326) at approximately 11:35 a.m., Mr. Goodman returned to his room at approximately 11:40 a.m. and found his front entrance left wide open. The bathroom door was closed.

Mr. Goodman then yelled at the room attendant (Daniel) who was found working outside Room 1227/1229 area and was asked why his front door was left open. At this time, another housekeeping staff (Esther) came out of his bathroom and explained to Mr. Goodman that she was actually checking the cleanliness inside his bathroom.

As Mr. Goodman approached the writing desk, he realized that his blue bag containing the laptop computer, printer, and digital diary was missing. He then asked both housekeeping staff to look for it but to no avail. Finally he decided to approach the assistant manager in the lobby for assistance.

Mr. Goodman was rather concerned about the loss and decided to report it to the police. A limousine was arranged to take Mr. Goodman, accompanied by a bellboy, to the nearest police station at 2:00 p.m.

A Guest Property Lost Report has been compiled and case closed.

At the end of the shift, Jackie copied all documentation about Mr. Goodman's loss case to the department heads concerned, i.e. Rooms Division Manager, Front Office Manager and Executive Housekeeper.

At around 6:30 p.m., Mr. Goodman approached the duty assistant manager and claimed that his lost items actually were taken by one of his colleagues, Mr. Tim King of Room 1232.

Questions for Discussion

1. Do you think Jackie Lai handled the incident appropriately? Explain.
2. If you were Jackie Lai, how would you have handled this incident?
3. What are the reasons to explain Jackie's failure to handle this case successfully? Suggest ways to prevent the reoccurrence of the mentioned mistakes in Question 1 above.

13

Effective Training and Communication?

Rosalie Wong

Company History

The Scarborough Corporation, based in London, operates an international hotel chain providing over 12,000 rooms in over 25 countries worldwide. According to the Chief Executive Officer (CEO) of the Corporation, the goal of the hotel group is to increase The Scarborough Hotels' leadership position in the upscale markets of the lodging industry. The CEO stresses that the goal should be attained by achieving superior consumer satisfaction through the quality of the services provided and the quality of personnel offering the services.

To ensure hotels in different countries can help to achieve the goal, the Corporation set standards for service and the quality of the accommodation. Moreover, detailed operation manuals, training films/slides and instructional aids for hotel personnel are also provided. Representatives from the headquarters will conduct an inspection to each property once a year.

The Scarborough Hong Kong

The first Scarborough Hotel in Southeast Asia was opened in December 1995 in Central, Hong Kong. As the first Scarborough Hotel in Southeast Asia, the hotel is positioned at the five-star level. Target business mix of the hotel is 65% business travellers and 35% leisure travellers. The hotel has 310 guest-rooms, all attractively furnished. The hotel's strategy is to offer a superior product to its customers at a reasonable price. The Scarborough Hong Kong also contains four food and beverage outlets, an indoor swimming pool, a fitness centre, a large ballroom and three medium-sized meeting rooms.

The Scarborough Hong Kong management team is mainly expatriates and reports to the corporation headquarters in London. The management structure of The Scarborough in Hong Kong is decentralized.

The Front Office

Since the front office is the focal point of the hotel, it is important to ensure that standards expected of the hotel are attained. As a result, Nicholas Brown from the United Kingdom was transferred to the position of the Front Office Manager of The Scarborough Hong Kong.

Nicholas, a very diligent man in his late twenties, graduated from a famous hotel college in the United Kingdom. He started his career in the hotel industry after graduation when he was only twenty-one. Within six years, as a result of his outstanding performance and diligence, he was promoted to the Front Office Manager in a five-star hotel, The Scarborough Manchester. Therefore he is always proud of himself.

The Front Office of The Scarborough Hong Kong, including Nicholas, consists of twenty staff. Figure 1 shows the organization of the front office. Among the team, six have more than four years' front office experience, seven have been in the industry for not more than one and a half years, and the rest are fresh graduates.

Nicholas is an experienced Front Office Manager. He realizes that front office employees play a vital role in the creation of a positive first and final impression of guests, and in the establishment of an on-going rapport with guests. Moreover, quality services can only be delivered when his staff are well-trained and have knowledge about the property and guests' needs. Therefore, Nicholas stresses the importance of training and good communication within the front office.

All training programmes are conducted by Andy Chan, the team leader and trainer of the front office. Andy was the chief receptionist of a four-star hotel, The Delta Hotel, which was closed down in the

Figure 1: Organizational Chart of the Front Office

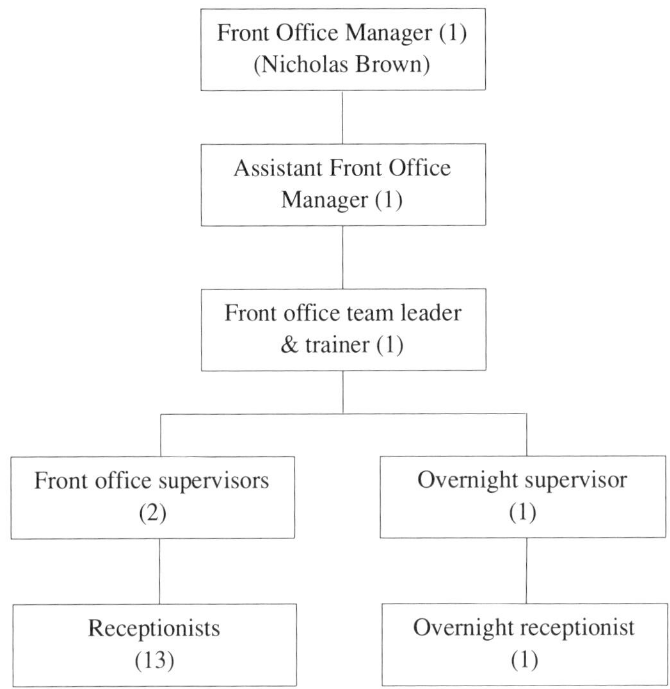

beginning of 1995. Andy was instructed to make use of those training materials and instructional aids which were provided by the corporation headquarters. Moreover, Nicholas also encourages Andy to convey the empowerment concept among staff at the front desk. To illustrate the empowerment concept, Nicholas seldom questions Andy's decision and training programmes.

To ensure the uniformity of the job procedures and the services provided, Andy conducted the same type of training for all supervisors and receptionists.

Since the grand opening of The Scarborough Hong Kong, the operation of the front desk was quite smooth. Minor problems were unavoidable, but there had been no serious complaints received. Nicholas thought that the training programme provided by Andy was very effective and the communication within the front office was also good.

The Incident

One day, Nicholas was informed by the Marketing Department that Royal Florists (an international tour company) had decided to hold the annual meeting in Hong Kong and would like to stay at The Scarborough Hong Kong from 23–26 February 1996. The group consisted of 280 guests.

After careful consideration, Royal Florists' reservation was accepted. Royal Florists is a good tour company with potential to provide business for the hotel in the future. Moreover, The Coachtrans group, consisting of 300 guests, was scheduled to check out from the hotel on that day.

As Royal Florists is a potentially good business contact for the hotel in the future, all front office staff were briefed that special attention should be paid for the group. In order to ensure smooth operation, all rooms for Royal Florists group were pre-blocked well in advance. No blockage of these rooms could be moved. Andy was appointed as the person-in-charge of the group. All receptionists, except one supervisor and two receptionists, were scheduled to be on duty on 23 February.

However, it was a busy day on 23 February at the hotel because many guests were checking out of the hotel and Royal Florists group would be beginning to arrive at around 3:30 p.m. In addition, there were many arrivals (especially early arrivals) on the day and one of the staff was on sick leave. Since some staff were fresh graduates and not very experienced, Andy was also busily engaged on checking in early arrival guests.

Andy only had the chance to check the status for those blocked rooms for the group at around 11:30 a.m. Unfortunately, he was shocked to find that most of the rooms have not been checked out yet. To understand what had happened, he called the housekeeping order-taker to investigate the situation immediately.

After fifteen minutes, the housekeeping order-taker informed Andy that there were "Do Not Disturb" signs on the doors of many expected check-out rooms (The Coachtrans group). Moreover, one of the guests told the housekeeping staff that he had permission to stay in the room until 3:00 p.m.

At around 3:30 p.m., the lobby of The Scarborough was jammed with group people who were checking out and checking in. Andy tried his best to check in the arrival group guests; however, only 25% of the rooms blocked had been released by housekeeping. Therefore, a great deal of noise was created. Nicholas was only alarmed at this time by this nasty situation. In order to control the situation, with no other alternatives, Nicholas decided to send waiting guests to coffee shop and lounge in the hotel. Nevertheless, the lobby was too noisy and no one could even hear a word from Nicholas.

Finally, at around 8:00 p.m., all guests from Royal Florists were checked in. Nicholas got very annoyed with Andy about his carelessness. Also, he would like to find out who offered the late check-out for The Coachtrans group.

Nicholas sank down into a chair at the back office after this long day. Accidentally, he noticed a thank-you note addressed to Justina (a new receptionist who is recently graduated from a university). The message read as follow:

Dear Justina,

Thank you for your kind assistance in arranging the late check-out for my group.

Hope to see you again in Hong Kong, Bye!

John Morrison
Chairman of The Coachtrans

The next day after the incident, Justina was questioned by Nicholas regarding the late check-out issue of the Coachtrans group. Justina recalled that the night before the group's departure, the Chairman requested the late check-out for his group as their flight would be leaving in the evening. Justina claimed that she was unaware of any reason not to grant the request for late check-out and therefore late check-out at 3:00 p.m. was offered.

Conclusion

Originally, Nicholas thought that the operation of the front office was running smoothly in The Scarborough Hong Kong. Moreover, his staff were all well-trained and there was good communication within the department. However, the Royal Florists' incident made Nicholas changed his thought. Since representatives from the headquarters will conduct an inspection to the property next month, Nicholas is now thinking what he should do to rectify the situation.

Questions for Discussion

1. What are the inherent weaknesses in the front office management of The Scarborough Hong Kong?
2. Suggest ways to rectify the inherent weaknesses in the front office management.
3. What do you think about the causes for the mentioned incident?
4. As the Front Office Manager, what are your recommendations or appropriate actions to overcome the incident?

Part V

Human Resources Management

14

Continuous Employment?

Simon C. K. Wong

XYZ Hotel is a three-star hotel located in Tsim Sha Tsui. It contains 300 rooms and three outlets, namely coffee shop, bar, and a small function room accommodating around 150 persons for meeting. The hotel has 180 employees.

The Food and Beverage Manager, Peter Cheung, supervised a workforce of 80 employees. Because of the current economic recession, the business for the function room was poor; its rental income dropped drastically. The normal rental rate for the whole function room is HK$3,000 per hour. Currently, the occupancy level of this function room is around 30%.

The hotel owner, James Tang, decided to redevelop the function room into a mini shopping arcade. In order to fully utilize the space and maintain a stable income (i.e. shop rents) for the hotel, this function room will be redeveloped into around ten shops. The rental charge of each shop will be around HK$30,000–80,000 per month. The overall objective of the hotel owner is to maintain a stable monthly income of HK$600,000.

In this connection, General Manager Lawson Chen called up a working committee comprising:

- Food and Beverage Manager, Peter Cheung;
- Personnel Manager, Susan Chow;
- the Controller, Victor Ma; and
- Chief Engineer, Philip Sze.

After the meeting, an action plan was drafted as follows:

Date	Action	By
1 March 1996	Hold booking for function until 30 April 1996	Food and Beverage Manager
1 April 1996	Reassign labour to other outlets by Transfer Prepare Redundancy package for staff who are not needed. Decide which staff to be laid off.	Personnel Manager, Food and Beverage Manager
1 May 1996	Vacate the function room. Redecorate the function room to become a shopping arcade. Sales Department or Estate agency be responsible for soliciting shops tenants.	Chief Engineer, Sales Director, Controller
15 May 1996	Sales to solicit shop tenants. Tenancy agreement signed.	Sales Department, Controller
30 June 1996	Decoration of shops completed.	Chief Engineer
1 July 1996	Shops tenants move in.	Sales Department
1 August 1996	Grand Opening — Ribbon Cutting. Promotion — Lucky Draw to attract visitors. Promotion — To in-house guests.	All concerned

The action plan was agreed with all concerned. Everyone was happy with the schedule. Originally, the manning of this function room was two supervisors plus six full-time waiters. In times of good business, part-time waiters will be employed. For the past six years, three part-time waiters had been hired for this function room.

The two supervisors and three of the six full-time waiters were transferred to the coffee shop. One full-time waiter was transferred to the bar. Finally, the Food and Beverage Manager agreed to lay off the remaining two full-time waiters.

After discussion with the Personnel Manager and the Controller, a redundancy package was drafted for the full-time waiters:

1. One month's payment in lieu of notice.
2. Severance Payment (Formula: two-thirds of monthly salary $\times$ years of service, provided they work in the company for more than two years).

3. Any outstanding leave owed to employee, such as annual leave, statutory holidays.

4. Provident Fund — Staff contribution plus company portion in accordance with the rules of the company's Provident Fund scheme.

On 1 May 1996, after the last day of banquet function, Susan Chow received a letter from the Labour Department. In the letter, it stated that three part-time waiters claimed they should receive the same compensation benefits as those being redundant. The three part-time waiters were:

1. Chan Sui, aged 45 (work from 1991) — He had started to work as a part-time waiter in 1991. He performed very well and also lent a hand whenever there was no casual labour. He always showed up and had good punctuality records.

2. Wong Ah-man, aged 38 (work from 1992) — He worked as a part-time waiter on the referral of Chan Sui. He worked usually three days in a week. However, sometimes his attendance fluctuated. Rumours said that he had a full-time job as a life-guard in public swimming pool.

3. Chiu Sin-kwok, aged 35 (work from 1988) — He joined the company as a waiter in 1988. However, he resigned after one year of service. He was called back to work as a casual waiter in the Banquet Department in the evening. He was in fact also working as a part-time waiter in the Room Service Department of another three-star hotel. In this arrangement, he could earn more money than a full-time waiter.

After collecting some background information from the Food and Beverage Manager, the Personnel Manager discovered that no official records were available to prove their attendance to work as part-time waiters in the function room.

However, it was a fact that these three gentlemen had been working for the hotel as permanent part-timers.

On 6 May 1996, reporters from a television broadcasting company suddenly approached the Personnel Manager and the Food and Beverage Manager to get more information about the redundancy issue.

On 10 May 1996, the Personnel Manager received a letter from a union leader claiming that he represented the three part-time waiters in a claim for the full settlement of their redundancy package. The union demanded that the hotel management discussed the whole issue with them. Otherwise, industrial action or demonstration would be carried out.

On 17 May 1996, the hotel security discovered that some flyers and protesting papers had been adhered to the staff entrance of the hotel.

The Labour Department had scheduled a reconciliation meeting on 15 June 1996 for both management and the part-time waiters to resolve the dispute.

The General Manager called an urgent meeting with the Steering Committee members to handle all these matters. The hotel owner demanded a quick action plan to resolve the whole issue.

If you were the Chairman of this Steering Committee, how would you handle the whole situation?

Questions for Discussion

1. Do the three part-time waiters have the right to sue you in terms of full redundancy compensation?
2. What evidence must management find in order to win in the Labour Tribunal?
3. Casual waiter is very common in the hotel industry in Hong Kong. Is the "Continuous Contract: 418" concept applicable to this case?
4. Can you suggest a "mutual" proposal that would satisfy both parties? If yes, what benefits or compensation you will include?
5. How would you handle the mass media for your hotel as a tourism property?
6. Union influence is not strong among the hotel staff. There is not any staff union in your hotel. In this case, how would you handle the union leader?
7. In future, what advice would you give to the hotel management in order to reduce the chance of having this kind of labour disputes?

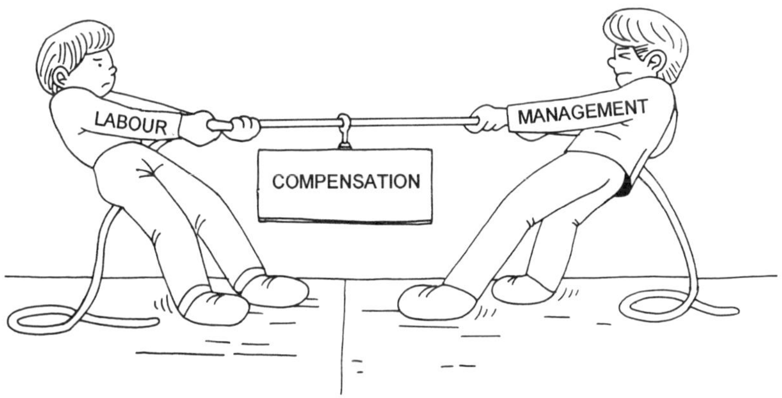

15

The Airport Limousine Team of Crown Hotel

Sylvester Yeung and Catherine Cheung

Two hotels in Hong Kong, the Kowloon Crown Hotel and the Hong Kong Crown Hotel, both belonged to the same hotel management company, the Crown International Corporation based in Boston, the United States.

Heated discussions have been going on between the General Managers of the two hotels on how they could cooperate in cutting costs. Among the topics of joint purchasing and recruitment, one of the proposals was to combine the two originally separated airport limousine service counters into one under the name of "Crown Hotels." After restructuring, the new counter would be under the direction of Eric Wong, the Airport Manager of Hong Kong Crown Hotel. The Airport Manager of Kowloon Crown Hotel, Alan Cheung, who possessed lesser experience, would be reappointed as Assistant Airport Manager.

Figure 1:   Management Structure of Crown Hotels

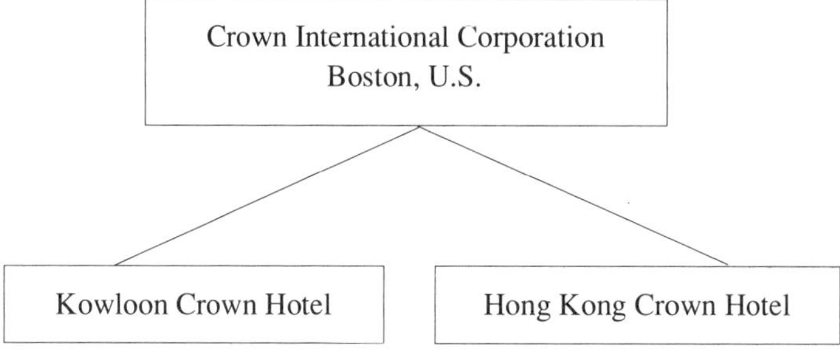

Figure 2:   Original and New Structure of Crown's Limousine Service

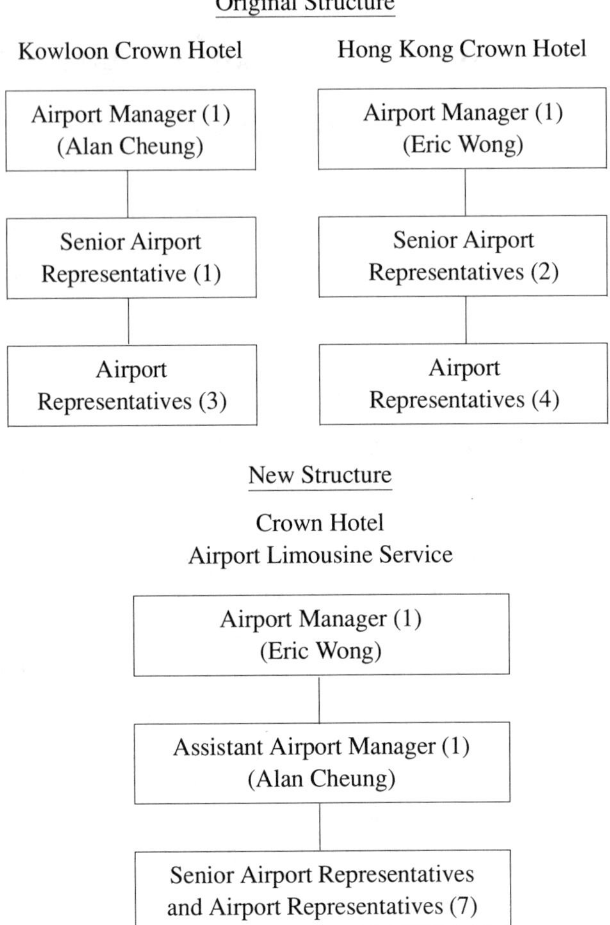

With this move, the total number of airport representatives of the two hotels would be reduced from twelve to nine. Nine employees would be working under the newly combined counter while other work arrangements would have to be made for the remaining three airport representatives.

To implement the change, the hotels offered the following two options to all airport representatives:

1. To work under the combined counter with the same title and compensation and benefits. (However, apart from Eric Wong and Alan Cheung, a maximum of seven employees could choose this option.)
2. To be transferred to hotel front desk as receptionists with the same compensation and benefits.

However, one of the airport representatives of Kowloon Crown Hotel, James Chan, refused to work either under the combined counter or to be transferred to front desk as receptionist. James rejected the first option on the basis that he did not want to work under the supervision of Eric Wong as he claimed they did not get along too well. James also rejected the second option as he claimed he was computer-illiterate and would not enjoy the job nature as front desk receptionist.

He further argued that although the two hotels were under the same management company, the Kowloon Crown Hotel was owned by the Tan family in Singapore while the Hong Kong Crown Hotel was owned by the Richardson family in Hong Kong. Therefore, working under the new structure was indeed the same as working for a new employer. He claimed that the Kowloon Crown Hotel was in breach of contract and quoted a labour ordinance to back up his position: a dismissal by reason of redundancy occurs when the requirements of the business for employees to carry out work of a particular kind in the place where the employee so employed cease or diminish, or where they are expected to cease or diminish.

At that moment, he earned a monthly salary of $9,800. Since he has been working for the hotel for over five years, he claimed the following compensation:

1. Long service payment,
2. Severance payment,
3. One-month payment in lieu of notice from hotel,
4. Outstanding annual vacation,
5. *Pro rata* bonus.

However, Sylvia Law, Director of Human Resources of Kowloon Crown Hotel, rebutted the claim by stating that a dismissal by reason of redundancy did not stand when an employee had been dismissed by a company employer and a re-engagement offer had been made by an "associated company" of the original employer. The offer, in this case, is treated as though it were made by the original employer. Furthermore, James would not be considered dismissed as he unreasonably refused an offer of employment on the same terms or on terms that were no less favourable.

Sylvia had been working for the Kowloon Crown Hotel for more than twelve years. She had started as a Personnel Officer and because of her outstanding performance, had slowly worked her way up to the present position. She was independent, determined and professional. She felt that James was trying to take advantage of the situation.

Before dealing directly with James, Sylvia made some internal inquiries and investigation. According to comments made by other colleagues, Eric was well-known for his high demand on staff performance and behaviour while James' performance was said to be only fairly satisfactory. James has been late for work a few times and was even once complained of by a guest for his rude behaviour. However, these were all covered up by Alan as they had known each other since high school. It was indeed Alan who recommended the Personnel Department to employ James. Also, by looking at James' personal file, he had attained a Form 5 education level but ever since his first day of work in this hotel five years ago, had no record of taking any part-time studies or attendance of training courses. Sylvia concluded that James lacked initiative and desire for advancement.

Despite this, James filed a severance payment claim in the Labour Tribunal against his employer, the Kowloon Crown Hotel.

Questions for Discussion

1. How can the two hotels handle the transition smoothly?
2. Does the case justify a redundancy situation? Do you think an offer of re-employment is being unreasonably refused?
3. If the case is finally judged as a termination by reason of redundancy, what should the compensation be?

4. If the case is finally judged as a termination of contract by the employee and not a redundancy situation, what should the compensation be?

16

The Opening of the Seaview Hotel in Taiwan

Sylvester Yeung and Catherine Cheung

The Seaview Hotel Taipei (SHT) was due to open in December. With 550 rooms and 20 suites, the luxurious commercial hotel had about 700 staff. The hotel is targeted at business travellers. Since this was going to be the first hotel in Taipei which had international standard facilities, the management expected the service to be of world-class quality.

Karen Lee, Director of Human Resources of Seaview Hotel Hong Kong (SHHK), was instructed by the Director of Human Resources, Asia Pacific of Seaview International, to recruit a management team to support the opening of the new hotel. In addition, Karen had to select a senior front office employee from Hong Kong to be transferred to Taipei as Assistant Front Office Manager.

Quality service could only be achieved through well-trained staff. Unfortunately, service awareness and standards in Taipei were relatively low due to their lack of exposure to world-class hotels. SHT was to be the flagship of international hotels in Taiwan. Karen knew it was going to be a difficult task to train the local employees. Therefore, she understood that her selection of the supporting team members from the SHHK would be a critical factor to the success of the opening of the SHT. Rooms Division and Food and Beverage departments would need the most support. She learned from the Personnel Manager of Taipei earlier that the English standard was poor among the general staff. Therefore, Karen felt that an English native speaker had to be seconded to Taipei to teach English.

Finally, she had produced a members' list as shown in Table 1.

Table 1:　Members of Staff from Seaview Hotel Hong Kong

Name	Position	Department assigned
Mabel Ip	Chief Accountant	Accounts
Peter Chan	Assistant Manager (Coffee Shop)	Coffee shop
Andrew Lau	Reservations Manager	Reservations
John Wong	Training Manager	Training
Mark Washington	Sous-Chef	Kitchen
Christina Lee	Assistant Manager (Executive Floor)	Executive Floor
Sharon Ryan (English native speaker)	Reception Manager	Front Desk

The duration of the secondment for the members was three months. It was also agreed that on top of their regular salaries, a 25% hardship allowance would be given to each of them.

Clarence To, the Front Desk Manager of SHHK, was given the job of Assistant Front Office Manager. His background was listed as follows:

- Age : 27
- Education : Finished his part-time studies in Hotel Management in one of the vocational schools in Hong Kong
- Marital status : Single
- Language ability : Fluent Cantonese, fairly good in English and Mandarin
- Experience : Worked his way up to Front Desk Manager from a receptionist nine years ago; technically competent in Front Office procedure and operation

In terms of the compensation package for Clarence, Karen had decided to adopt the home-based policy. This approach linked Clarence's base salary to the salary structure of the relevant home country. Apart from the provision of annual round-trip air tickets and entitlement of 24 days' annual vacation, it was agreed that housing and taxation were to be self-financed. Since the duration of his overseas assignment was two years, she thought this policy would assist repatriation.

The General Manager of the SHHK had expressed his concern that sending the key staff members away might directly disrupt the normal operation of the local hotel. However, it was a corporate directive and Karen had reassured him that they would be seconded for only three months and that staff members would be there at different times so as to minimize any possible lack of staffing in Hong Kong.

Karen had asked her secretary to prepare all the necessary arrangements for the secondment. A formal letter of invitation together with a brochure briefly describing the culture and environment of Taipei were sent to each of the supporting team members. The purchase of air tickets and the issue of visas were being taken care of.

Things seemed to be going smoothly. However, a few months later when Karen visited Taipei to check the progress of the supporting team, she unexpectedly discovered that the team members were indeed not working harmoniously with the local employees there. Obviously, conflicts and misunderstandings had occurred between them on several occasions. Motivation and morale of the team members had dropped to a low level.

The Sous-Chef, Mark, had communication problems with the local chefs there who hardly spoke any English. In many cases, the chefs misunderstood Mark's instructions and Mark began to lose his temper and patience. At one time, Mark even left the workplace in the middle of the shift. Cultural differences also surfaced when Mark suggested that they should not use too much garlic on staff meals, especially to frontline employees, as it would create bad breath. The kitchen chef ignored his suggestion, defending that Taiwanese love garlic and strong-flavoured food.

There was also argument between the local Executive Floor Managers, Mona Wang and Christina. Mona saw no reasons why Guest Relations Officers could not sit down and talk to guests or even accept invitations from guests for drinks after office hours. It was culturally accepted in Taiwan. However, Christina insisted that professionally and ethically speaking, no hotel staff should accept any invitation from guests. A social distance should be maintained between staff and guests.

Even the supporting team members were not on good terms with each other. John had designed a thorough training plan for the Front Office Department but was told by Sharon at the last minute that she would conduct all the training sessions. John had felt that Sharon was trying to take all the credit from him. Role conflicts were obvious. Since then, both of them had rarely talked to each other.

The morale and spirit of the team members started to get low. Grievances and complaints were their common conversation. It was most difficult for the local junior staff. They got stuck-in-the-middle between the local management team and the supporting team. To whom should they listen?

Another major problem facing Karen was Clarence, the newly transferred Assistant Front Office Manager. No doubt, Clarence was doing a fine job in his new capacity. However, he seemed to have difficulties in adapting himself to the new living environment. He complained about the high cost of living in Taipei as he was responsible for his own accommodation expenses. He also disliked the traffic conditions, the terrible air pollution and the generally slow sensitivity and living pace of people. Because of these problems, he seemed to bog himself down at work, working almost sixteen hours a day and stayed in his small nearby apartment most of the time after work, not socializing with his peers or making any friends. Very soon he started to miss home and his friends in Hong Kong. He had talked to Karen of the possibility of either going back to Hong Kong as soon as possible or readjusting his compensation package. Yet, Karen claimed that the position of Front Desk Manager in Hong Kong had already been replaced.

Karen was wondering if she had made a wrong choice of transferring Clarence to Taipei. Apart from competence and technical skills and knowledge, what factors had she overlooked?

As the day of opening of the new hotel was approaching, Karen was thinking how she could remedy the situation.

Questions for Discussion

1. Was the secondment successful? How could you, as Karen, make it successful?

2. Do you think Karen did not find the right candidates to help out the opening? Comment on your response.
3. What are the factors that led to the conflicts between the local staff in Taipei and the supporting staff?

Part VI

Marketing Management

17

The Falling Star Hotel

Rosalie Wong

The Hotel

The Panorama Hotel in Tsim Sha Tsui was built in 1992 by ABC Company which leased the hotel at the time to MHD Corporation, an eight-year-old U.S.-based hotel management company. MHD is responsible for the operation of approximately twenty properties in the United States, ranging from three-star to five-star hotels. The arrangement between MHD and ABC consisted of a six-year contract which specified that the Panorama is a five-star hotel, and that MHD will receive 5% of the total revenue earned by the hotel as a management fee. All employees in the hotel are employed by MHD. ABC will pay for all capital expenditures including the renovations being carried out on the property.

The General Manager of the Panorama Hotel had previously been employed as General Manager and a resident manager of a four-star hotel in the United States. Besides that, the management team of the Panorama is mainly expatriate and well-qualified. The style of management is bureaucratic, which for the most part is accepted by the rank and file, and staff do what they are told. New ideas are seldom solicited within the organization, and problems are individually handled as they arise.

In anticipation of the business, meetings and convention market, the Panorama Hotel is positioned as a commercial hotel at the five-star level. It has 500 guest-rooms, five food and beverage outlets specializing in different cuisines, some being popular with business travellers and business persons in the town, a ballroom with a capacity of 450 persons, and six sophisticated meeting places. There are two Executive Floors in the Panorama which makes the hotel eminently suitable for business travellers. Each room on these floors is uniquely decorated and supplied with an electric shoeshine machine. Executive Floor guests also have exclusive use of a clubroom, equipped with a wide-screen television and a stereo system. Moreover, guests are invited to a complimentary continental breakfast in the morning and to evening cocktails and canapés in the clubroom. In addition, the Panorama also has a business centre which provides expert staff and most of the business services to ensure that travellers' business is conducted in the most efficient manner.

The Business

Since its opening, the Panorama has been known for its exceptional food and beverage, as well as its efficient and friendly staff. The hotel was considered as "upgrade, classy and a hotel with ambience." Its selling points were the Executive Floors and the high level of service and attention provided. During the first two years, the occupancy level of the Panorama has averaged 84%, while the occupancy level for other competitive hotels in close proximity has been approximately 88%. The clientele of the Panorama Hotel has consisted primarily of guests from the United States, Germany and the United Kingdom who were in town on short-term business. The guest mix is 70% business travellers and 30% pleasure travellers.

Unfortunately, with newly opened hotels and the on-going renovation of some other hotels, there appeared to be an increasing supply of hotel rooms for business travellers in the area. This has negative impact on the Panorama's occupancy level. In order to maintain the occupancy level and be profitable, the management team of the Panorama was forced to rethink the strategy.

Research was carried out by the sales team to evaluate the demand for hotel rooms by various market segments. The result revealed that the business segment would grow steadily in the coming two years as a number of conferences, exhibitions and large-scale events have been booked. Also, the tourist segment is expected to increase in size. The construction of several new theme parks by the government and different constructors recently is an evidence of this trend. However, this segment is looking for hotels which can provide the proper package, i.e. the lower-rate one.

In order to meet the fierce competition in the business segment, the management team finally decided to change the Panorama's marketing plan. The Panorama made more attempt to attract tourists and group business by creating some attractive lower-rate packages.

After the Change

Within the recent year, owing to the increasing number of tourists and groups, the Panorama successfully maintained its occupancy at the level of 80%. However, this level was not acceptable by management. The Director of Sales of the Panorama reported that there was still considerable market resistance on room rates, and that to be competitive, rates have had to be further reduced in order to bolster the occupancy.

With a further drop in room rates, the occupancy increased by 3%. The guest mix of the Panorama has been changing towards a higher percentage of pleasure travellers and groups, many from Asian countries and Europe. The change in guest mix has had some effect on overall hotel operations. For example, more tourists can be found crowding around the information desk for arranging tours and seeking information; some meeting places have been arranged as a venue for group check-in; more extra beds have been needed as triple occupancy is a common group pattern. Besides that, the change in guest mix also has affected the business of some food and beverage outlets. The business of the coffee shop has been brisk, especially at breakfast, as most of the seats has been reserved for groups. Some pleasure travellers love to patronize the Chinese restaurants for dim sum and dinner.

However, with the shift in the market, front office personnel found that they could not get their work done efficiently due to constant interruptions by guests and telephone enquiries. Housekeeping employees claimed that the rooms were much messier than before, and that it was harder to clean up the room after guests left and to get the room ready to let within the pre-set time. Besides that, most staff experienced difficulty in understanding the message of some of the guests as these guests spoke English with different accents or even spoke some unfamiliar languages.

Pleasure travellers commented that most staff of the Panorama lacked warmth and a friendly attitude.

On the other hand, business guests also complained that the hotel had become too noisy, making it more difficult for them to get their work done. For example, groups usually gathered at the lobby before they departed for sightseeing and thus created a great deal of noise in the lobby. Besides that, business guests always found it difficult to get a table at the coffee shop for breakfast, and the Chinese restaurant is no longer an ideal place for business persons. They claimed that the overall environment and ambience of the Panorama had changed. Moreover, service now is only just adequate.

Outlook

At this point in time, the Panorama Hotel remains marginally profitable. However, projections for the coming two years do not look promising. The ABC Company has already hinted the possibility of an early termination of the management contract unless the profitability is improved. Besides that, the failure of the Panorama's management to maintain the standards of a five-star property as specified in the original agreement is another charge which may be used by the owner for breaking the contract.

Questions for Discussion

1. What do you think about the management strengths and weaknesses of the Panorama Hotel?
2. Do you think the decision (to change the marketing plan) made by the management is beneficial to the hotel?
3. If you were a member of the management team, what would be your recommendations for the new strategy?

4. What are the existing problems on the quality of service? Suggest ways to rectify the problems and to maintain the service standards?

18

The Star Chain

Paul Leung and Catherine Cheung

Eugene Kao is the Managing Director of a well-established hospitality chain, The Star Chain, in Hong Kong and Mainland China. Late last night, he gave you a call regarding a strategic decision they have to made within the next two days. As the Chain's newly employed business and marketing consultant, Eugene presented to you all the information he has on hand and asked you to give advice. Eugene has emphasized that time is a critical factor. A decision has to be made on Friday morning. You glanced at the clock on your table top. It is 11:30 p.m., Tuesday night.

After hanging up the phone, the attached information came over the fax.

Company Background

The Star Chain is a hospitality chain formed in the early 1960s. The founder, L. Cho, is the grandfather of the current Chief Executive Officer, W. S. Cho. The company is owned and ran by the family for the last thirty-five years until very lately, Eugene Kao, an outsider, was employed as Managing Director.

The Star Chain started with a small restaurant serving high-quality European cuisine. The operation is well perceived by customers and soon diversified into different operations, such as Chinese restaurants, bars and clubs, and hotels in the Asian region. In the early 1980s, the Chain started its first operation in Mainland China under the open door policy. Because of the founder's family background and contact, L. Cho has chosen Shanghai as the stepping stone to enter the China market. Five years later, the second hotel was established in Beijing. Currently, the company has five hotels all over China and W. S. Cho is planning to start operation in other Asian countries.

The Decision Background

The hotel operation was profitable in the 1980s and the early 1990s. Now, the tight economic policy and the keen competition all add up to make the business less attractive. W. S. Cho therefore decided to close down the operation of one of the two oldies and renovate and expand the other.

More information is given as follows:

The Shanghai Star

A 100 rooms' four-star hotel targeted at leisure tourists, the hotel was found in 1980. Owing to the ageing of facilities and the core premises, the renovating and expanding cost is estimated to be much higher than the Beijing counterpart. Capital cost is estimated to be US$750,000 with 5% ups and downs.

The Beijing Star

It is a 130 rooms' four-star hotel targeted at the business segment. The capital cost for upgrading it to a five-star hotel is estimated to be around US$400,000 with 15% ups and downs.

The facilities of the two hotels are shown in Table 1.

In addition to the capital expenditures, closing down either one of the above-mentioned operations will involve certain redundancy cost, development cost and other charges. Details are shown in Table 2.

The effect of closing any one site will be the elimination of 180 manual labour and 50 administrative and supporting staff. The labour cost saving is estimated to be HK$200,000 for both cases per month.

Table 1: A Comparison of the Facilities of Shanghai Star and Beijing Star

	Shanghai Star	Beijing Star
Executive floor	Nil	Nil
Swimming pool	Yes	Nil
Bar	Yes	Nil
Gymnasium	Nil	Yes
Business centre	Nil	Yes
Fine dining restaurant	Yes	Yes
Ballroom	Yes (capacity: 350)	Yes (capacity: 150)
Room service	Yes	Yes
Laundry	Yes	Yes

Table 2: A Comparison of Closing Down Shanghai Star and Beijing Star

	Closing Shanghai Star	Closing Beijing Star
Redundancy cost	HK$500,000	HK$350,000
Run-down cost*	HK$150,000	HK$200,000
Relocation of staff	HK$100,000	HK$ 80,000
Loss on sales of assets (other than land)	HK$ 95,000	HK$150,000
Income from sales of land	US$25,000,000	US$18,000,000

* Run-down cost refers to the operating overheads for closing down the hotel other than redundancy and relocation of staff.

The income from sales of land was the best estimates obtained from a local property agent in Shanghai. The estimate for Shanghai is quite accurate with about 5–10% deviation. The Beijing estimate, however, might deviate with error up to 35%.

Table 3 shows the business performance of the two hotels.

A minutes of the management meeting is also shown in Table 4.

Table 3: Business Performance of Shanghai Star and Beijing Star

	Shanghai Star	Beijing Star
Average rate per room night	US$60	US$85
Standard deviation of room rate	US$1.75	US$3.45
Annual turnover (room nights)		
1986	36,500	39,859
1987	36,125	40,537
1988	36,250	44,567
1989	32,798	36,789
1990	36,500	47,050
1991	35,500	46,535
1992	35,800	41,756
1993	36,028	45,201
1994	36,123	39,987
1995	36,454	43,333
1996 (projected)	36,500	44,250

Table 4: The Management Meeting Minutes

Date : 13 May 1996
Time : 5:30 p.m.
Venue : Board Room
Present: Mr. W. S. Cho, CEO
　　　　　Mr. E. Kao, Managing Director
　　　　　Mrs. F. Chan, Marketing Manager
Subject : Regional Redevelopment

The purpose of this meeting was to decide which of our two four-star hotel should be closed and torn down.

Mrs. Chan mentioned that our Shanghai hotel is the foundation of our operations. Emotionally, she was quite reluctant to have it close down.

Mr. Kao agreed with reservation. He had the concern that the physical condition of the Shanghai premises is ageing and out-dated. The renovation cost would be much higher than the Beijing alternative. Furthermore, Beijing is the capital of China. It would be good to maintain the foothold there.

Mr. Cho asked Mr. Kao to prepare a situation analysis and to present his recommendations to the board on Friday's board meeting. Decision should be left to the board to vote.

The meeting adjourned at 6:00 p.m.

Questions for Discussion

1. Based on the information provided, what is your recommendations to Mr. Kao? Why?
2. Other than the options mentioned, is there any other alternatives available to The Star Chain?
3. What other tools can be utilized to assist your decision making?

Class Adoption

We shall provide a free inspection copy to each teaching professional who is interested in reviewing our titles in this series for adoption in his courses. Supplementary materials, such as Teaching Notes, will also be provided free if the titles have been adopted. However, The Chinese University Press reserves the right to refuse request for complimentary copies which are not within its complimentary copy policy.

For inspection copies, please write using your institution's letterhead indicating your class size and the intended adoption date to:

Business Manager
The Chinese University Press
The Chinese University of Hong Kong
Sha Tin
New Territories
Hong Kong
Telephone: (852) 2609 6508 / 2609 6500
Facsimile: (852) 2603 6692

MANAGEMENT DEVELOPMENT SERIES

Forthcoming

Hong Kong Management Cases for Supervisors

Hong Kong Management Cases in Human Resources Management

Hong Kong Management Cases in Information Systems Management

Already published

Hong Kong Management Cases in Marketing

專業管理叢書

即將出版

《管理人經濟學》

《管理學原理》

已刊書目

《香港商業法》

《組織行爲與人事管理》

《管理資訊系統》

《數量方法的管理應用》

Annual Case Writing Competition

Write to Win

Since 1988, The Management Development Centre of Hong Kong has started organizing the Annual Case Writer of the Year Competitions. With the sponsorship of the American Chamber of Commerce Charitable Foundation, the competitions have been most successful and attracted a large number of good quality case submission every year.

For further information about the Case Writing Competition, please call or write to the Executive Officer of The Management Development Centre of Hong Kong at 11/F., VTC Tower, 27 Wood Road, Wan Chai, Hong Kong (Tel: 2836 1816, Fax: 2572 7130).

The Case Study Group of Hong Kong

The Case Study Group of Hong Kong was formed in 1987 with the objective of promoting case method for management teaching and training in the territory. With administrative and advisory support from The Management Development Centre of Hong Kong, the Group has regular meetings and seminars during which cases are presented.

The Case Study Group is open to those in Hong Kong who are involved in the use of case materials and methods in management training and development (whether by occupation or interest).

If you will complete the details below, we will add your name to our mailing list and notify you of all forthcoming activities.

Name (Last, First):	
HKID No.:	
Job Title:	
Company Name:	
Company Address:	
Home Address:	
Telephone (office):	
Fax (office):	
Specialized area:	

Please return to:
Ms. May Li
The Management Development Centre of Hong Kong,
11/F., VTC Tower, 27 Wood Road, Wan Chai,
Hong Kong

Tel : 2836 1818
Fax : 2572 7130